Altcoin

A Best Book to Know Digital Currency Bitcoin

(Cryptocurrency Ultimate Money Guide to Crypto Investing)

Elvie Zboncak

Published By **Jackson Denver**

Elvie Zboncak

Altcoin: A Best Book to Know Digital Currency Bitcoin (Cryptocurrency Ultimate Money Guide to Crypto Investing)

ISBN 978-1-77485-929-2

Legal & Disclaimer

The information contained in this book is not designed to replace or take the place of any form of medicine or professional medical advice. The information in this book has been provided for educational and entertainment purposes only.

The information contained in this book has been compiled from sources deemed reliable, and it is accurate to the best of the Author's knowledge; however, the Author cannot guarantee its accuracy and validity and cannot be held liable for any errors or omissions. Changes are periodically made to this book. You must consult your doctor or get professional medical advice before using any of the suggested remedies, techniques, or information in this book.

Upon using the information contained in this book, you agree to hold harmless the Author from and against any damages, costs, and expenses, including any legal fees potentially resulting from the application of any of the information provided by this guide. This disclaimer applies to any damages or injury caused by the use and application, whether directly or indirectly, of any advice or information presented, whether for breach of contract, tort, negligence, personal injury, criminal intent, or under any other cause of action.

You agree to accept all risks of using the information presented inside this book. You need to consult a professional medical practitioner in order to ensure you are both able and healthy enough to participate in this program.

Table Of Contents

Introduction

An effective transaction between buyers and sellers is key to any business's success. Both sides benefit from the implementation of the process. Ancient economists created the physical system for payment to validate the entire process.

The advancement of technology forced entrepreneurs to consider online platforms, as studies revealed that their target audience spends most of their time online.

The digitalization of the transaction was needed to allow them to conduct business efficiently in the global market. This digitalized commerce can be both transparent and incorruptible.

In 2008, Satoshi Nakamoto published his white paper. The idea of Bitcoin was born. It offered investment opportunities for ambitious businesspeople. Bitcoin was invented during this time.

This electronic cash system utilizes the peer to peer network system to reduce double spending during transaction processes. These great inventions were a relief from the failure of all the centralized attempts. This cashless payment system eliminates the possibility of forgery after confirmation of the transaction.

The cryptocurrencies have had revolutionary results. It was named the "Dawn of a new industry" because it is based on the prediction that all nations around the world would make cashless transactions within their respective regions in order to minimize the inconveniences of physical transactions.

The fact that the payment system is unmanipulated preserves and increases its value over the long-term. This media proves to be a convenient and fast way to pay across the globe. The system's private and anonymity allows it to work for outlawed economic activities, such as the black-market.

This ecosystem of coins and tokens is highly volatile, so global investors may consider investing. While the risks involved in investing can lead to the loss of their investments, the most fortunate investors have the ability to boost the value of the coins up to 1000% within a few days. This high-tech invention leverages the Okcoin, shapeshift and poloniex exchanges to allow for the easy trading of hundreds more cryptocurrencies. Economic studies have shown that the coins are more valuable than major European stock-exchanges.

The Bitcoin remains the most widely used cryptocurrency. However, global investors and users continue to keep their eyes

3

open for other cryptocurrencies that could expand their investment opportunities. Waves NEM, Waves NEM, Dash, Monero are just some of the cryptocurrencies.

These chapters would help readers understand other cryptocurrencies. This virtual monetary unit is not represented in any physical form and can be divisible into 100,000,000 "Satoshis."

Before investing in cryptocurrency, new Crypto investors will need to establish portfolios. It is difficult for them, however, to decide on which assets to include. A $119.673 portfolio is an option for risk-taker investors depending on their individual income. The investors can select the amount of coins to be invested based on the investment goal.

Your portfolio's success depends on the place you buy the coin, how it is traded and what coin you choose. For the best protection of your investments, however, it is important that you use the best apps for tracking your portfolio.

Simply buy Bitcoin and send it over to an exchange. The exchange can then be used to buy any other coins you are interested in, making a fortune from trades.

A crypto portfolio requires investors to take risks. The risk-taker considers using risk-reward formulas to determine how much risk they are comfortable taking. This then influences which coins they want to invest in. Economists recommend that investors invest at least 50% of their capital in safe coins such as Bitcoin, Monero, and Ethereum. Due to the ever-increasing price of the coins it is important to determine the entry point. If the coins are low, ambitious investors might consider entering the trade. The predicted increase in coins' value at the end 2018, and for the future, makes it a good time to invest in coins.

To find the most trending and highly valued coins in the marketplace, conduct regular research. It is important to keep your cryptocurrencies safe.

The unique features of cryptocurrency wallets make it convenient to secure our coins. The wallets make sure that the coins' values are maintained regardless of economic fluctuations.

Investors have many choices and must decide which wallet best suits their needs. The market offers many options, so it is important to evaluate them all before making a decision. This will ensure that global investors don't lose any of their hard-earned capital.

Trezor is one of many available wallets. Diverse tools are also available to track your progress, and the prices and current values of the gold coin.

Investors who are focused on maximizing their returns in cryptocurrency should be aware of technical analysis and investment advice.

The collected information includes the latest crypto news like historical price data and market prices. Despite the commercial benefits, investing in cryptocurrency can result in losses.

This is why it is crucial to consider both the negative as well as the positive aspects of ecommerce before investing in trending coins of gold.

These chapters provide insight into the whys and wherefores of investing in this type business. They also explain how to choose the right coin for you investments.

It is worth taking the time to read this book in order to fully understand this investment. This will ensure that you can make the right decision and secure your hard-earned money for an enjoyable experience in this kind of online business.

Chapter 1: Building A Crypto Portfolio

Global investors may consider diversifying their assets across many asset classes to minimize their risk exposure. Because there is less risk, entrepreneurs can make a lot of money from their investment.

To create a long-term successful portfolio, however, there are several steps that must be followed. Global users have the option of building a long or dynamic portfolio depending upon their goals. The long-term portfolio can be compared to retirement, while the dynamic portfolio lets the user trade cryptocurrencies however they like.

This chapter describes the steps that are required to establish a successful cryptocurrency portfolio. It will also provide an overview of how to make the investment process memorable. Before you invest in the best cryptos, it is important to know how much you can afford to lose. The economists suggest that investors not take on more than what they can afford.

Once you have decided on how much to invest in cryptocurrency, the next step would be to devise a diversification plan. This would involve spreading across all top cryptocurrencies (or 5-10) that are available worldwide.

This precaution protects against coins that are highly popular or with high trading volumes. In addition to the security, diversification gives the risk taker the ability to learn about the entire cryptocurrency marketplace.

This understanding helps veteran investors realize high returns while risking their hard earned cash. The success or failure of the chosen coins will determine how much the user adjusts the holdings. A portfolio entry can be made efficient by using three blocks: position sizing, research and entry price.

1. Research

The cryptocurrency world has many exciting and complicated elements that an investor must understand before they put their money to work. Research is therefore an important concept in cryptocurrency investments. It allows gamblers to not only identify the best coins that they should risk their money on, but also the payment methods available for cryptocurrencies and the best wallet to choose from. For those who want to make big investments, it is essential that they do a pre-assessment.

Many online platforms make it possible to conduct studies on economic strategies for the benefit of the digitalized people. Analyzing coins means identifying their creators.

Before setting up a portfolio for enhanced online commerce, you need to be familiar with the basics of blockchain technology. For maximum output, it is important to follow the recommendations in various publications.

2. Position sizing

You are doing extensive research to find out the market condition. It's important that you make sound investment decisions.

After the analysis, the next step is to decide what action you want to take. With the market information and the best coin to choose, you can now decide on how much to invest with the intention of making big returns. The most successful investors spend a lot of money on coins that will present them with fewer risks than the alternatives.

For the best possible decision on choosing the most profitable coins, you can attach either the Medium, Low or High rating to each coin. Then, rationalize the position size.

Each rating represents a percentage from your total investment. You are free to choose the percentage you're comfortable with regardless of what percentage is displayed. A lack of knowledge about the risk that you are taking is why professionals recommend investors put a small amount of their hard-earned capital. For goal-oriented depositors, it is also difficult to decide the risk level of their investments due to fluctuations in coin prices. It would be prudent to only invest five percent of your resources if you intend to invest 10 percent. The remaining portion can be saved for future investment. This reduces the likelihood of inventors suffering losses.

There will be an ups and downs in the prices of coins, so it is essential to be flexible while building your portfolio. Regular manipulation of these platforms will allow you to achieve maximum results from your wise decision.

3. The entry point

The key to the success of your business is the selection of the right coin, as well as the amount and time required to do so. Although you may be certain that your gold coin will make money, professional economists that specialize in this type of business advise that it is not wise that you invest all of your resources in them.

The fluctuating price of coins means you could experience losses, even with the most popular coin. In a matter of months, the Bitcoin-USD graph will experience wild runs, including significant corrections and minor recovery phases.

This discovery means that the entry time or the time when you decide to make a capital investment on the coin is key in predicting the expected returns.

There are important differences between buying coins at the top and in a dip. You need to apply your technical skills including critical analysis of historical resistance levels and support levels before you can make predictions regarding future prices.

Due to the poor history of resistance and support levels, you will have to draw your personal conclusion. But, if you are only here for a short-term adventure this prediction criterion will not be essential. Historical analysis can be used to determine whether trading in the coins is subject to high volatility. You will need to decide the best wallet for your purchase once you've made your investment. The next chapter covers the many wallets available.

Chapter 2: The Best Cryptocurrency Money Wallets

It is crucial to have a digital wallet that allows for the safe and efficient transfer of digital currency. The software program stores both public and private keys. This allows for easier interaction with different blockchains.

The cryptocurrency wallet doesn't store currency in a physical location, unlike the traditional wallet. Instead, it stores records of transactions. This program allows users to check their balance, send money, and regulate all other functions that make up the blockchain technology.

The system works by having an individual send you the gold coins and sign off that he or she owns the coin to your address. To use digital coins and unlock funds, your private keys must match the public currency address.

There are many wallets that you can choose from, giving you the chance to find the one that best suits what you like. This section explains the various wallets you have the option to choose from. It also explains how the digital marketplace works to make your experience with gold coins easier.

Once your public and private keys are matched, the balance within the digital market will rise while the senders fall. The program does not allow real coin transactions, however the transaction record in the blockchain and the changes to your balance in cryptocurrency wallet are indicators of the operation.

The process can only be made easier if the private and public keys match.

Many wallets can be used to store your digital currency and make it accessible. You can divide the wallets into three categories: hardware, software, and paper. These wallets can also be used online, on a mobile device, or both.

Desktop: The wallets are installed on a desktop computer or laptop. But, the only way to access the wallet is from the same computer that the digital wallet has been downloaded and installed. This wallet is one of the most secure for cryptocurrency. Problems arise when the computer gets hacked or is infected. If this happens, your funds could be lost.

Online: Unlike desktop wallets, these wallets can be accessed online from any computing device. Private keys are stored online and managed by a third party, making them more vulnerable to theft or hacking attacks. These wallets can be difficult to use, but they offer greater convenience for those who consider using them.

Hardware: These wallets save your private keys, other than the online and digital wallets. Transactions are performed online even though there is an offline storage option.

One advantage to this type wallet is its compatibility with multiple web interfaces. These interfaces can support different currencies, depending on which coins you prefer. To make it work, connect the device with any internet-enabled PC and enter a security password before you can send currency.

Once the transaction is confirmed, it's complete. Hardware allows you to make transactions faster and keeps your money safe.

Paper: This type of wallet offers high security for your currencies. This digital wallet utilizes software that secures the generation of a pair of keys, before they can be printed. It's easy to transfer your gold coins to your paper wallet.

The Bitcoin can be transferred by moving the funds from the software wallet to the public account on your paper wallet. Transfer your money from your paper wallet directly to the software wallet if you want to withdraw or spend the currencies. This can be done either manually via keying in your private key or automatically by scanning QR codes on your paper wallet.

The best wallets for cryptocurrency wallets.

Many wallets can be classified into these categories. The wallets are used to monitor your online transactions in order to reduce the chance of you losing your gold coins investment. While wallets are distinctive, there are some key traits that every crypto wallet must have.

The wallet must be affordable and come with minimal drawbacks.

You should verify that the company handling your wallet is not known for security breaches.

For the selection of your best choice, it is important that the wallet is easily accessible.

Users should find it easy to access their wallets and be able to quickly purchase any currency.

User-friendly wallets are essential

Design needs to be relevant for all users.

Professional economists advise that you choose a wallet with all the above-mentioned features for a more enjoyable online business experience.

A. Trezor Wallet

The hardware wallet is compatible with almost all operating system. The cryptocurrency wallet supports Bitcoin, DASH (Zcsh), Ethereum Classc and Bitcoin Cash as well as Expanse, Zcsh, Zcsh and Ethereum Cash among other ERC 20 tokens.

Trezor Wallet

B. Ledger Nano

This cryptocurrency wallet is very similar to Trezor. The hardware wallet supports multiple cryptocurrency. By simply pressing the buttons on the wallet, users can approve transactions before they are executed. This second security layer prevents sudden attacks from affecting the success of transactions. It is recommended that users use this wallet to store Ripple, Qutum and NEO.

Tratis and Starts are as important as the Ubiq.

The Ledger Nano S CryptocurrencyWallet

C. Exodus Wallet

This Exodus software wallet is compatible with personal computers. This wallet includes the ShapeShift utility, which makes it easy to convert or buy cryptocurrency with another user without having to leave the wallet interface. This wallet supports Bitcoins, Aragons, Augur and Dash.

The Exodus Wallet

D. Coinomi Wallet

This wallet supports the Android operating platform only. This wallet supports a large number of cryptocurrency assets. The wallet service provider is working hard in order to release the IOS version within the next few years.

The Coinomi Wallet

E. Jaxx Wallet

Experts claim that this wallet supports multiple currencies. The Decentral Company's digital wallet supports Ether Classic (Dash, Ether), Ether, DAO and REP, Bitcoin, and Litecoin cryptocurrencies. This wallet allows users to download it on both desktops and mobiles. It is not compatible with the Coinomic wallet.

The Jaxx Wallet

F. The Agama Wallet

The Agama Wallet, although still in its development phase, offers a unique feature that allows users the ability to use multiple cryptocurrencies. Users can also choose which security is most important for them. This wallet supports Bitcoin Dark (Litecoin), Unocoin and Zcash as well as Zcash, Dogecoins DigiBytes, DigiBytes,

DigiBytes, DigiBytes, DigiBytes, Digibytes, DigiBytes, DigiBytes, DigiBytes, DigiBytes, DigiBytes, Komodo, Zetacoin and the Bitcoin cryptocurrencies. Unfortunately, this wallet only works on desktops. Economists believe the mobile-compatible versions are yet to be released.

The Agama Wallet

These wallets are not the only ones that you need to have a great experience dealing with coins. These wallets are the Blockchain.info (an electronic wallet), Coinbase(online exchange), MyEtherWallet, PaperWallet, and the Electrum. Before you purchase any of these wallets, make sure to thoroughly research the options and determine which one is best for you.

Are Cryptocurrency-Wallets Reliable?

There are many wallets available that can protect your money. However, the security level varies depending on which type of wallet you choose and what service providers you use. Recent studies show that web servers have a higher risk of being compromised than the offline option. Even though online wallets have been shown to be most vulnerable, there's a few precautions that can help minimize the risk that users lose their hard-earned funds.

I. Ensure that your software is up to date

Keep your software current to ensure you have the most recent security features. It is important to keep your wallet software up-to-date. You also need to update any software you have on your phone or computer.

II. Keep your wallet safe

A large portion of your funds should be kept safe, and only a few coins for everyday applications can be found online, on your mobile, or in your computer. For backups, you have two options: cold storage or offline. Backups such as the paper, USB, or Ledger Nano can help protect your computer from failures. It also gives you the opportunity to recover your wallet if it has been stolen or accessed remotely by hackers.

III. You can add security layers

According to experts, the higher the level of security you have, the better. The password protection, for example is a way to keep unauthorized people away from your funds. Multisig transactions such the Copay or Armory are a good option to protect your funds. This type of trade requires permission from another user before it can be completed.

Chapter 3: Other Cryptocurrencies To Consider

The topic of cryptocurrency is hot in the world of online business. The viability and rise in value of Bitcoin over $10,000 is proof of its viability. The bitcoin market was worth $250Billion and the value is expected to grow even more.

The cryptocurrency market isn't just Bitcoin. By April 2018, there were over 1,500 currencies, which indicated a market size of approximately $330 million. The best part is that these altcoins can handle more transactions as Bitcoin can, and some are also designed to improve the user's security.

The problem is in choosing the best Bitcoin alternative. This chapter covers not only the main altcoins but also how to assess whether the alternative cryptocurrency makes sense.

Bitcoins

You must evaluate which cryptocurrency is best for your company to ensure you make the best decision regarding the choice of cryptocurrency. This assessment includes a range of factors that could help you choose the right alternative cryptocurrency to Bitcoin.

i. Development activity

Reviewing every cryptocurrency's development activity is one of the ways successful crypto investors make their business a success. Goal-oriented people believe that a team that updates their products and patches bugs regularly is the best company.

Recent studies have shown that Bitcoin has one of the most active development teams. All work is publically available via the Github repository, making it easy for anyone to verify if any developer is not doing their job.

Due to the fact that all altcoins have been created from Bitcoins, regular updates are necessary in the event of a Bitcoin bug. This is because they share the same codebase and the bug will surely affect altcoins. It is crucial to choose the alternative cryptocurrency that has more updates to improve users' experiences.

ii. The innovation in technical and monetary rules

Although Bitcoin's limited production of 21 million coins has contributed to its rise in value, some view this as a problem. Alternative coins such the Dogecoin which has approximately 100 billion coins is expected to grow every year by 5.256 Billion coins.

This is a change in monetary rules that, unlike Bitcoin, encourages investors to consider altcoins. Different cryptocurrencies have used different innovations to benefit their overall ecosystem. This makes altcoins a good choice.

iii. Public interest

Popularity of the coin is crucial in deciding which cryptocurrency alternative to invest in. For this purpose, you can simply search the name for the coin on Google or Bing. Its popularity will be indicated by the number of hits. There will be millions of search results for established coins. Alexa also allows you to find out how popular a coin's official website.

iv. Market capitalization

Coins with low market capitalization are easy to manipulate, leading to scam coins. These altcoins could expose you to the possibility of losing a lot. It will be much harder to manipulate coins with larger market capitalization, as it would require significantly more capital to alter the prices.

V. Community strength

In the end, coins that aren't part of a group will be ineffective as no one will use them. It can be hard to determine the number users for a particular coin due to its decentralized nature. However, it is possible to use proxy measures to estimate the community's size. Proxies can be used to estimate the size of the community using proxies such as Reddit activity or Facebook likes.

vi. Vi.

In order to decide whether or not you should buy altcoin, it is necessary to monitor the trading activity. The alternative cryptocurrencies must be purchased as it is traded by many people.

The Solidest and Most Obvious Altcoins You Can Invest in

There are many options for Bitcoin. Here are some common coins that crypto investors might find valuable:

1) Ethereum

The Blockchain technology has been enhanced by the addition of this coin, which was originally proposed by Vitalik Buterin (a Russian programer) in late 2013. This cryptocurrency allows smart contracts and makes trades subject to conditions. This coin currently trades at $500 and is expected increase in value as the years progress. This coin is second in the rankings of analysts to Bitcoin.

The Ethereum altcoin

2) Ripple

Altcoin, which has a market capitalization of $26.3 million, was created in 2012 to facilitate trade settlements rather than a trading frenzy. It is currently in circulation at 38 billion Ripples. This altcoin's value has remained stable over time as commodities are moved across water bodies. Ripple is distributed, and not like other currencies, by ripple Labs of San Francisco, the coin's creators.

The Ripple Altcoins

3) Bitcoin cash

This cryptocurrency was launched in August 2017 in an attempt to alleviate the burden of Bitcoin users by reducing the cost and complexity of transactions. The market capitalization of this coin is approximately $12.9 million. Bitcoin Cash uses the exact same mining technique as Bitcoin.

Bitcoin Cash

4) Litecoin

This coin, also known by the "silver to Bitcoin's gold" moniker, has a market worth of $7.3 billion. This cryptocurrency is a distributed network that handles trades quickly.

The Litecoin has a more frequent update to its blockchain than the Bitcoin. This means that it can use the Scrypt algorithm for mining on computers rather than the expensive graphics systems required for Bitcoin. Analysts claim the altcoin is priced at the same level as the Bitcoin.

The Litecoin

5) Dash

This coin was first introduced in 2014 as an XCoin based upon the Bitcoin technology. It currently has a market worth of around $3.0 million. This coin has its own cryptocurrency and mining system. The cryptocurrency provides features for instant transactions, called InstantSend, as well as private transactions, called PrivateSend. The "nodes," and the more powerful "masternodes", enable both these properties.

Dash Altcoin

There are many altcoins you can choose from so it's important to conduct extensive research to find the best alternative cryptocurrency to use for your hard-earned funds.

Chapter 4: Choosing The Best Bitcoin Currency To Invest In

Analysts in Economics predict that the demand for cryptocurrencies will continue growing, and that individual coins will have a higher value over time. Based on the current indexes, which show how crypto investment outperforms hedge fund investments within the stocks, this prediction is made.

There are many coins to choose from so it's important to research the various gold coins before you make a decision on which cryptocurrency you want. This chapter covers the most important factors that should be taken into consideration when selecting the best cryptocurrency to invest in.

Before buying or investing in gold coins, you must determine exactly the problems they are trying to solve. This determines whether the cryptocurrency is long-term viable. The value of the coin will depend on its users' desires. To properly consider the coins, you must have a clear view.

Crypto investors should consider investing in coins with real value according to professional economists. Visionary investors should consider cryptocurrencies that focus on the world as more valuable.

Your chosen coins should be dealt with by companies that have a long-term perspective to ensure you are able to benefit from their value for a longer time, and therefore increase your profit rates.

Review some of the comments left by other users about the coins. These will help you to predict what you can expect to get from investing in your chosen coin. Knowing this information gives you the ability predict the coins that will remain valuable for years to come, and the ones that will lose their value.

It is determined by the amount of competition among the coins which one to invest in. Due to the existence of coins that solve similar issues, it is essential to examine this aspect. It is not wise to select a coin to solve an issue without considering other coins with the same purpose. Visit the websites of the coins in order to see if the design is professional or not. Make sure to investigate any potential security issues that either coins may be exposed. To avoid potential inconveniences down the road, it is worth testing the software.

Consider all of these factors to determine the best approach for solving global issues that could affect the livelihoods of residents in the jurisdiction.

The best cryptocurrency to invest is the one that has the maximum supply and float. This is an advantage for long-term cryptocurrency investments.

Bitcoin for instance can only have 21 million coins. This determines its demand as well as supply. Once all coins are mined the supply will decrease and the demand will increase, thereby determining the price. However, the 100,000,000 Ripple coins ensure that the coin will continue to be relatively inexpensive.

There will be the same amount each year of Ether which will ensure an endless supply, thus lowering its price. The price of each coin is determined by how much demand there is and how much supply there are. Bitcoin is the most precious of all coins.

It is important to determine whether cryptocurrencies are available for purchase. A currency that is accessible on big exchanges so that many people can access it has the potential to see a rise in value.

A currency's difficulty to obtain is not enough to disqualify it from your consideration. After doing thorough research, any coin can be considered. When choosing the best coins, the most successful investors look at the availability of those coins.

The same applies to new users. This is a way to ensure a successful business intervention. For determining whether an investment is successful, you must consider the storage options available for the coins. Expert investors will consider how easy it is to store the coins when choosing which coin they should risk their hard-earned capital. For your convenience, the preferred wallets should be simple to access.

Another important factor in determining the success or failure of cryptocurrencies is marketing. Although cryptocurrency is decentralized and community-owned, it still requires marketing in the same way that Apple Company continues to market its high-quality products.

According to studies, there were many brilliant ideas that didn't materialize because of poor marketing strategies. You should also consider the cryptocurrency whose developers are determinedly to market.

This can be done by checking their social media channels. The role of online influencers in promoting currencies you wish to invest in is another important consideration. Evaluating the marketing of each currency is crucial, since economists state that their success hinges on effective marketing.

Scam coins have been used in numerous cases since the introduction this form of business. You should however, consider the following options to lessen your chances of becoming a victim of this fraud:

It is important to have information that can be confirmed about the person who owns the coin. It is important to choose coins whose development team includes known members from the cryptocurrency community.

You should verify which escrow holds the coins for customers, until they have completed a set deal.

It is not a good idea to consider projects that do not have any code-related link.

Be cautious with projects that make bold claims on their products. Avoid cryptocurrencies with low market capitalization or low trading volumes.

You need to conduct extensive research in order find valuable currencies, while also avoiding the swindle coin.

Chapter 5: Less Obvious But Good Future Prospects

The third chapter of this book describes the trending and common alternative crptocurrencies to Bitcoin that new crypto investors can choose from. Altcoins are considered the best alternative to Bitcoin. These altcoins offer huge returns for experienced crypto investors who have realized large profits from their investments. The coins are also popular with new users who believe they are worth the risk.

The above-mentioned altcoins are just a few of the many gold coins. It is a smart decision to invest in these coins based on their value. This chapter describes ten less well-known altcoins. It also explains why they are worth investing in for a bright future.

1. The ARK Altcoin

The ARK altcoin, which has seen a sudden surge in value is sweeping the crypto markets. This gold coin was the third most valuable crypto currency, having risen by 19.28% over 24 hours. This altcoin offers an all-in-one, blockchain solution. All you need is the "Point." Click. Blockchain" for more advanced blockchain technology.

The wallet of altcoins supports all major operating systems on the desktop as well as the Android and iOS mobile devices. This gold coin uses the Delegated-Proof-of-Stake (DPoS) consensus mechanism made of up to 51 delegates spread worldwide, with the aim of running the ARK network for a block reward. This strategy seeks to multiply the number of users.

To avoid the reliance on the DPoS mechanism the ARK group is trying to integrate multiple programming langauges into the system. This will ensure that many developers are considering using the ARK. Unfortunately, altcoin has a declining value, and the ranking is now at 49th. Despite the prediction that the crisi would continue in the future, the transparent, determined ARK team make this a worthwhile project. This advantage that ARK enjoys over other cryptocurrencies confirms that the ARK's Reddit forum has surpassed the 20,000 subscriber mark recently. SmartBridge is considered the most appealing feature to boost this altcoin by the ardent supporters.

Altcoins ARK

2. The NEO Altcoin

NEO Altcoin is one blockchain platform that facilitates development of smart contracts. The NEO altcoin also allows for the creation of digital assets, similar to Ethereum. To enhance investor experience, the platform uses two different tokens: Gas (for gas) and NEO (for NEO).

NEO claims that the project's main objective is to use smart contracts as a decentralized, distributed platform to manage non-digital assets. Apart from opening a bank, you can pay your rent via the smart contract each month.

This China's response on Ethereum aims to bridge that gap between traditional and digital assets.

Altcoin was ranked 20th in 2016 after its debut. It achieved a $5billion market value by the close of 2017 (2017). American economic research predicts that the NEO Market will grow at 32% annually by 2023. Media attention is an important factor in the NEO currency's success.

The headlines were the driving force behind the price rises of NEO. NEO is not as responsive to regulations as Monero and Dash. However, the developers are openly stating their willingness to cooperate with the authorities.

The NEO altcoin

3. The OmiseGO crypto

The OmiseGO project was developed on the Ethereum platform in 2013. This OmiseGO cryptocurrency is much more than an altcoin. Users have the option to use it to boost their online trading.

This project connects existing cryptocurrency wallets and the OmiseGO central blockchain to replace the traditional buying or selling of gold coins from exchanges. The "Unbank the Banked" slogan is used by the open payment platform. Its primary objective is to provide better financial service for the global population. At the moment, cryptocurrency is ranked at 19th place with a market cap of $1,506,964,404. It has been valued at $14.77 for this year (2018) by experts who expect it to continue growing in value.

The OmiseGO Altcoin

4. The IOTA Altcoin

The Tangle technology is what makes the IOTA currency different from other coins that use Blockchain technology. This technology addresses the concerns of security, scaleability, and fees. This Tangle, which is unable to support time dependent Transactions, cannot be used by financial institutions.

This cryptocurrency, MIOTA on the exchanges, is all about Internet of Things. With more consumers using connected devices, it's all about the Internet of Things. The IOA hopes to become the cryptocurrency that supports machine–to-machine transactions in the universe. All machines that are connected to the network serve as the nodes for verifying transactions. The responsible team for tis' development claims that the cryptocurrency is not tamperproof but secure.

The IOTA Altcoin

5. TheTenX Alcoin

This digital currency allows users to access the cryptocurrency anytime and anywhere they like using a debit/credit card connected to a mobile application. This project aimed to connect the existing virtual and physical platforms. Many businesses and users are struggling to make use of this infrastructure.

TenX Card (a debit card) is owned by investors in this digitalcoin. This TenX Wallet facilitates payments. The cards can be used in approximately 200 countries and have more than 36,000,000 points of acceptance. TenX's partnership with the major credit cards firms is what has made the card so successful.

This project uses the COMIT Route Protocol and Cross-chain Pay Channels to award users the opportunity to use the Blockchain assets. TenX is the premier liquidity provider to offer real world payments.

The TenX Card

6. The Neblio Altcoin

This digital currency is one of the most valuable cryptocurrencies. It currently has a market worth of over $150 million. The market cap for this coin is around $176 millions. The Binance account accounts for around 97.3 per cent of the total volume.

The availability of Neblio Github is an economic indicator that advises crypto investors to look into this coin if they wish to see huge returns from their investments.

The Electrum Lite Wallet was released. This project also introduces an Android app with a Neblio iOS application submitted for Apple Company approval. The program's success gives the digital community a boost.

The Neblio Altcoin

7. Steem Altcoin

This decentralized cryptocurrency runs on Steem blockchain. This technology also powers the Steemit platform for blogging and social media. This digital coin is not mineable, and the technology just allocates the tokens to the reward funds to be paid to Steemit users.

The coin is also used for digital peer-to–peer payments. This 2016 release boasts a market cap of approximately $1.5 Billion, placing it in the top 25 most valued cryptocurrencies. This product can be traded at the top cryptocurrency exchanges, including the Poloniex.

Steem Altcoin

8. Private Instant Verified Transaction (PIVX), Altcoin

This digital coin was launched as a DASH coin product back on January 31, 2016. However, the difference lies in the consensus method used by the PIVX. While the Proof of Stake (PoS), is used by PIVX, DASH uses a Proof of Work (PoW).

The Zerocoin protocol is used to improve the privacy features of the PIVX currency. The primary goal of this coin, aside from the increased privacy, is to exchange fast and efficiently. Analysts warn that this coin could be used for criminal activities because of its privacy emphasis.

This coin is extremely volatile, with a rapid increase in its value and trading volume. PIVX has an estimated market capitalization of $191 millions and about $1 million in daily trading. A unique feature of PIVX is its light-weight Quark algorithm which works with very little energy.

The PIVX altcoin

9. The Loopring Altcoin

This open source, decentralized exchange protocol boasts a market cap of approximately $50 million. Coin prices are at 0.65 each to make it more attractive for future growth.

The growth potential of the coin makes it the best choice for crypto investors. This product's technology was developed to eliminate counterparty risks and reduce dependence on centralized third party. It also improves liquidity via an order pooling mechanism.

In September 2017, the price of this gold coin on Binance was $0.055 which indicated a slight growth rate. A public set of smart contract that is responsible for trade and settlement can be found in the product.

This release is unlike other decentralized trading protocols in that it can mix and match orders. The loopring solution utilizes both the open smart contract and the unique assortment of decentralized actors. This allows it to fulfil the different functions of the looping network.

The Loopring Altcoins

10. The NULS altcoins

This customizable blockchain is important for both long-term as well as short-term investors. NULS altcoin separates the blockchain into many modules account, storage and ledger, to improve its reliability.

This coin provides smart contracts, cross-chain consensus and the multi-chain mechanisms. This coin is a promotion of the use blockchain technology in the business world.

According to economists it is worth considering investing in this digital cryptocurrency due to its small market capitalization of $55million. It is therefore a promising investment. For crypto investors looking for additional income, this coin could be a great investment.

The NULS Logo

This chapter covers ten coins. But, many more coins are unknown and have been proven to be the best platform for digital investors.

Therefore, it is important to research thoroughly to determine if you are interested in a digital coin that could make you rich.

Chapter 6: Tools For Investing Or Trading Cryptocurrencies

Blockchain technology gives investors the possibility to make millions by investing in the internet. Economists assert that success is a result of a simple idea. Then, they go on to create billions for their respective stakeholders.

This technology makes it possible for crypto investors make huge money after they decide to invest in trending cryptocurrency. These tools help you to identify the best cryptocurrency and other tools help you track your cryptocurrency portfolio.

This chapter describes the various tools that can be used to assist new users. It is essential that you do thorough research before you download and install any apps that will help you manage your cryptocurrency business throughout the season.

A. CoinGecko

Although it is still in biometric evaluation, (BEAT), testing, this tool proves to have immense value for both cryptocurrency traders and investors who want to compete for the small market.

This platform ranks cryptocurrencies across multiple exchanges. It allows you to view your preferred cryptocurrency's real-time price and the percentage change or decline during a transaction session.

The platform also includes the analysis of the market capital of different cryptocurrencies, as well as insight regarding the development or community activity of each coin to prove that its developers are still backing it. The community activities revealed how each cryptocurrency had a strong community.

b. The cryptowatch

While many of the tools can be useful in searching for the best places to buy gold coins or the best markets to buy them, this option allows you to improve your trading results once you have purchased your desired cryptocurrency. This gadget provides live feeds that provide information about hundreds of different cryptocurrencies on all eight exchanges.

Investors in different regions of the world are able to view the live feeds on cryptowatch which shows the movements of cryptocurrencies around the world. This advantage allows them to pick the right coins based upon the stack against the respective currencies. This tool can be used to predict the outcome of your investments in the coins of your choosing.

c.

This application allows investors to keep track of their cryptocurrencies, their investments and their equities. The tool offers regular reports that show your portfolio. This makes it convenient for you. The tool offers two options for accounts: the free version is available to newcomers, as well as the premium account that allows you to explore the importance of this cryptofolio.

Premium account owners have access to more features than the free account owners. But not every investor or trader needs all of the premium features. Users who want to access the premium feature must pay an annual charge of around $240. However, this fee is subject to fluctuation over the years.

The cryptofolio will accept payment in Bitcoin or Litecoin. For proper cash management, it is recommended to download this application and install it on your device if you enjoy the technical solutions and the notifications.

d. Cointracking

This company helps you to monitor both the gains and losses in your portfolio. They can also help with making adjustments to maximize profits while minimizing negative returns. This tool is both available online and on the desktop. It's free for everyone.

TabTrader

Mobile cryptocurrency portfolio users can use this tool for managing their investments. TabTrader mobile applications support a dozen different exchanges.

Unfortunately, this tool does not allow you to access smaller and foreign currencies. This tool works flawlessly on mobile devices. But, widgets that display currency values might be a little slow and cause inconveniences from time-to-time.

Professionists believe that a simple force closure of the app is enough to fix the problem quickly. This app is free for all users and comes with no additional cost for extra features, making it convenient to investors new to this online business.

f. BlockFolio

This most popular portfolio management tool supports both Bitcoin as well as the other altcoins currently available. You can track your investments throughout the entire process.

This tool allows you access to both the complete overview of the portfolio and the exchanges on each coin trade. You can also access the news section, which is one of the most impressive features offered by this option. The detailed price notifications allow you to easily look at the various altcoins prior to making a decision to invest. Following the fluctuation in prices, this notification is vital.

This tool has the order book and stock charts for all currency trends worldwide. BlockFolio, with all its important features, is my recommendation. It will give you a much better experience working in the business.

g. 3Commas

3Commas is a powerful trading tool for cryptocurrency. This device allows you to minimize risks and maximize profits.

This platform was launched in 2017. After you register, you'll be eligible for a $10 bonus. Once you have registered, you will be allowed to trade with the top cryptocurrency exchanges currently in trend, including Bittrex (Binance), Poloniex (Bittrex), Kucoin and Bitfinex.

This platform uses the API for connecting to the cryptocurrencies that you like. This API key must be set to disable withdrawals. This will protect your funds from any fraudulent actions. Smart Trading property permits investors to use both the Stop loss and Take profit to maximize their profits while minimizing the loss they may sustain.

The StopLoss will be set when coins prices fall below the standard price. While the TakeProfit tool automatically closes if you have reached your targets in terms profit, To enhance your cryptocurrency business, you should consider using this tool.

In addition to the unique tools described above, the economists advise investors to use the Bitcoin or Ethereum trending coins to gain the funds necessary to purchase the other coins crowding the universe.

The Coinbase, and the Coinhouse are two of the fastest accounts to ensure you get your coins as soon as possible.

Before you make your decision, Altcoin's subredditis, YouTube channels and r/cryptocurrency accounts of Crypto-traders, CoinMonsta as also as the CoinMarketCap can provide you with all necessary information. Therefore, you need to do thorough research to identify the tools that will give you an advantage in the market based on your preferences.

Cryptocurrencies to buy

This book will inspire you to read more about investing in altcoins. The experience will not be enjoyable if you do not know how or where to buy cryptocurrency depending on your needs.

Many media are available to purchase your coin. This allows those with bank accounts to enjoy the ease of purchasing their products. The direct wire transfer allows them to purchase the coins with cash using a credit/debit card, PayPal or the swap cryptocurrency.

If you do not have the money to purchase coins, you could also earn them as payment. There are many ways that you can convert fiat currency into crypto. You can also trade gift cards to Bitcoin on some of these sites.

You should make sure that your wallet is ready before you purchase any cryptocurrency. Without a wallet, cryptocurrency holders could become victims to hackers and potentially lose much of their hard-earned funds. To help you get the cryptocurrency you want, here are some options:

I. The Bitcoin ATM

Bitcoin ATMs are becoming increasingly popular around the globe. To be able to process the transaction, you must physically appear at the physical location. These machines are also useful if you want to buy altcoins. The majority of these systems will take your cash in paper before they give you a digital token.

The Coin ATM Rader offers a map and a comprehensive list of ATMs in all countries. Since most ATMs can only be accessed in big cities, rural areas are not able to access them.

A Bitcoin ATM

II. Buy.Cointelegraph

Cointelegraph recently partnered with Simplex to offer crypto investors the ability to purchase other cryptocurrencies, such as Bitcoin Cash and Ethereum with ease. Simplex accepts Mastercards and Visa cards along with debit cards and prepaid cards.

buy.cointelegraph.com

III. III.

LocalBitcoin.com is a great resource to find someone who is willing and able to transact the cryptocurrency. This is a great way to travel internationally, or for those who are unable to access crypto services.

IV. Coinbase

This is the most used service to allow the selling and buying of cryptocurrencies such the Ethereum, Litecoin, Bitcoin and Litecoin. This service is available to anyone in the world, with access from a dozen different countries. All states in the United States have access except Hawaii, Minnesota, Wyoming, and Minnesota.

Before purchasing your desired coins, first you need to download Coinbase on your smartphone or create an Account from Coinbase.com. After you agree to these terms, you will see a chart showing recent changes in the cryptocurrency market.

The next step is to select the purchase method that you prefer. This can be done by clicking the Buy button on your app or the Buy/Sell Tab on your website. To make small investments and quickly connect your debit/credit card, click on the Buy/Sell button. In the case of larger purchases, you can connect your bank account directly. This may take up to 5 days.

After you click the Buy button once more, choose the currency you wish to purchase. Next, enter the amount that you wish to spend in the U.S. Dollars. The total cost of the transaction, which includes the Coinbase small fee, will be displayed. Click the Buy button once again to confirm.

The Coinbase Exchange Company is the best way to buy the coins

V. Bitfinex

Another tool, this one is in use since 2012 for the purchase of cryptocurrencies. This website boasts to be the best platform for trading digital coins.

Both the iPhone and Android have apps that allow you to access services from wherever you are. Exchange trading, Margin funding, and Margin trade are three features that help to ensure its reliability.

Bitfinex has integrated the P2P finance market into Bitfinex, allowing both the lenders to offer advanced margin trading tools to the borrowers. This media has the advantage of providing a beginners guide to help you make the most out your experience.

In general

There are many ways to acquire your favorite coins and have a memorable online investment experience.

Why Cryptocurrencies are Not for You

The cryptocurrency market is a great way to make a profit, but it also presents risks. These are the main reasons long-term investors think discourage new users to invest in gold coins.

Speculative growth of your investment is possible

The prices of the coins are dependent on demand and supply, unlike traditional companies, whose growth is affected by turnover, earnings, and other internal factors. Your success rate in investing in gold coins can therefore be difficult to gauge.

The remittance problem

Many people prefer to buy coins for their curiosity than as a means of transacting. In Indi, the Reserve Bank of India warns people against investing in cryptocurrencies and declares that they are not trying to regulate the market. The gold coins can only be used to trade tangible assets in many countries worldwide, such as India.

Exchange rates fall and so does your money.

Due to the fact that many governments worldwide aren't willing to join the fraudulent bitcoin exchange it makes it risky for them to do so. Your money can be stolen or used to commit fraud. You are at risk of being involved in the trading and buying of the coins.

The banks have banned the purchase cryptocurrency using their cards

Citibank sent email notifications to clients, notifying them via email that they were unable to use their credit or debit cards to purchase the gold coins. SBI Card, India's second largest bank, has spread the news about the risks involved in investing in cryptocurrencies. Other banks and financial institutions followed the same path, which discourages new investors from investing in cryptocurrencies to make a fortune.

However, not all coins offer high returns.

Each cryptocurrency must limit the amount of coins it can issue. This prevents ambitious investors from making big returns. Be informed before you play with digital coins.

Chapter 7: The Vitality Of The Ethereumsmart Contract

If you're curious about Ethereum and its value, read this chapter carefully. An Ethereum is a distributed, ledger that makes it possible to transfer funds instantly using smart contracts. Ethereum will be much bigger than other blockchains, such as Bitcoins, that have blocks sizes of about one megabyte each. However, this technology will be used to replace older blockchains, which have a severely limited scalability.

A second feature of Ethereum is that it will allow its users the ability to run Smart Contracts on top. The Smart Contract will enable users to transact their business without the involvement of a third-party. Developers will also find ethereum a great protocol because it is open-source. Developers can easily create custom blockchains according to their needs.

Third, Ethereum provides developers with a means to create and publicly publish smart contracts. They have complete control over all transactions. Unlike other blockchains, such as Bitcoin and Litecoin which involve third parties in transaction processing, Ethereum does not involve them. A new transaction will be the only occasion when a third party may be involved.

We will again discuss the benefits of ethereum. Developers will be free to develop their applications on this highly developed platform. You can also publish your applications on the ethereum Main Net. The smart contract or programming code will be executed instantly after this has been done. This allows businesses to both earn income from their applications and protect themselves against losses. The use of Ethereum has many benefits.

Additionally, the future of decentralized applications will be brighter with the use and expansion of the Ethereum smart-contracts, ethereum, and other applications. Each company or organization no longer needs to depend on companies providing services via traditional servers and platforms. These companies can now simply offer the services required via the Ethereum platform. Through their smart contracts, they can offer their users the opportunity to communicate with each other via the most popular social networks.

There will be less delays with Ethereum technology. This is due to the use of the soon-to become widely-used proofof-stake method. The likelihood of a successful transaction is higher in this way. An additional benefit of using the Ethereum smart-contract is the ability to receive immediate updates. Because users will be able transfer their transactions through social media, they also have instant updates.

Recent developments in Ethereum technology have proven to be extremely promising. There are many reasons that entrepreneurs and developers are now taking advantage the Ethereum's advantages. More than a few developers are using Ethereum smart contracts to start their own businesses. This shows that the ethereum community still has much to do.

Additionally, ethereum will continue to gain popularity among entrepreneurs and developers, so we can expect more interesting and beneficial developments.

Why not invest in Ethereum tokens, ERC20.

It is clear that the hype around ethereum, and its ERC20 token, has reached fever pitch. Just by the name of it, you can instantly picture a world where technology, financial markets, as well as the internet, all come together. Investors, developers, industry leaders, government officials all seem to be interested in the ethereum revolution. What exactly is Ethereum, how does it operate, and what are its potential uses? Continue our discussion about the crypto currency that seeks to fix the problems in the traditional money transfer process.

This anonymous currency combines various elements of distributed computation such as Distributed Ledger Technology(DLT), proof based proof–of computational authority ("POW tokens"), and smart contracts between people may sound complex. But the coins combine many of the best parts of each of these elements to create a highly scalable, efficient and scalable payment protocol.

Essentially, ether is a unique combination of currencies based on the open source programming code used in popular decentralized Internet technology like Proof-of Computing (DET) or Distributed Ledger Technology. Moreover, ethereum has a flexible design that allows the integration and use of many languages. It is a combination of all three of these factors that makes it one among the most attractive decentralized technologies.

The biggest attraction of ether, however, is the fact that users can transact in real-time. It allows instant payments to be made. Smart contracts let users specify exactly what they want money to do. This includes security fees, withdrawals, and more. Smart contracts can also specify when tokens may be withdrawn. Because transactions in the ethereum network are executed peer-to peer, it is highly valuable to have this ability to transact instantly.

Ethereum is not supported by all apps. Ethereum is still in development and many developers have yet create an official wallet for e Ethereum and/or an ethereum compatible web browser. This may seem like a disadvantage but developers will still be in demand to create these apps. If you have a web browser which uses ethereum, you can buy ether using ether tokens that are identical to traditional online currency.

One of the main attractions of ethereum, as mentioned above, is its compatibility with many wallets. The distributed ledger used by ethereum is more sophisticated than those of leading cryptocurrency, so its native mobile applications are likely to be the best in smartphone technology. This is a particularly attractive proposition for corporations that need to transact corporate finance on the move. Even though you don't necessarily need to have a mobile application for ether to take part in the global community of enthusiasts, this should be another strong reason for you to buy ether to help the future growth and development of the cryptocurrency. Ethereum is ripe for successful Initial Coin Offerings.

The bright future that ether holds means that the network supporting it will continue expanding its client list. The existing roster contains prominent venture capital firms and private equity firms. But, the network will continue to grow its client base as the world learns more about the protocol and its open source platform. It is best to wait for a few more months before you make any investment in this new technology. You can, however, invest in other currencies or projects that have a better track history for future success.

Another benefit of buying an Ethereum smart contract is the possibility to use the proceeds to buy additional tokens. This will allow you to increase your portfolio's value even faster than traditional ways of investing. The ethereum platform makes it possible to earn a return on your investment in just weeks. This is a vast improvement over traditional investments like stocks or bonds which can take years. The benefits of this are obvious when you consider how much money your career will save. Keep in mind that these markets can be very volatile. Depending on your risk tolerance or leverage, you could lose money if your timing is wrong. The upside of leverage trading is much higher than the risk. Dollar-cost Averaging is a good strategy for investing in cryptos, such as ethereum.

These are just some of the many reasons you should be excited to invest in the future for ethics and cryptography. The developers and users of ether are one step closer to making the protocol open-source so anyone can disrupt the financial industry's existing order. The future looks very bright for crypto networks like ETHEREUM, which is among the most advanced crypto technology platforms.

What is Cardano exactly?

Cardano is described by the ADA as a privacy currency. It is an open-source protocol designed to build on the lessons learned from the bitcoin/ethereum protocols. It was developed by experts in the fields of finance, cryptography, as well as computer science. It has many advantages over the other currencies in circulation, including traditional coins. It was created to complement the existing currencies.

Cardano runs on its own decentralized network, which is unlike other coins. Cardano does not depend on central banks to issue its coins. Instead, it relies on individuals called nodes. These nodes create the network that is Cardano. Smart contracts, which are built into the digital currency code, are used to perform transactions. This unique feature makes it the most private of all privacy coins.

Cardano's biggest selling point as well as why it's quickly becoming popular is its completely free pricing. Cardano offers a free service, which is unlike most coins, which charge high gas fees, and can make a business' bottom line unsustainable. Cardano, also known as "cardio", allows transactions to be sent without user interaction. This is in contrast to other platforms that charge per transaction.

Another advantage of the cardio project is its ability use multiple blockchains. Cardano can run across three networks using three separate, but co-operating servers called "zones". These include the Waves Platform and the SBI-e. All these networks can work together to facilitate Cardano transactions, which are performed in real-time. This makes Cardano the ideal project for businesses that do not want to raise additional capital.

Cardano's extremely competitive price is another strong selling point. Cardano is a unique ICO platform that charges a lower rate per trade. Even with all the work involved, which may raise the cost of the coin's currency, the current exchange rates are still reasonable and far below the average price for similar coins. This price difference is much more than the average of all coins.

Cardano's most distinctive selling point is the fact that it can operate on two different blockchains. The pre-mine is used as collateral for the security of the token. The pre-mine serves as collateral for the actual currency's security. Depending upon how you look at it, both sides have their advantages. Below is how the coin project works on both chains.

The premine is used to secure the execution of Cardano contracts. The Cardano Foundation holds the tokens, which cannot be fractionalized. You cannot exchange them directly with any person or entity. Instead, the Foundation issues tokens in a limited quantity and adds them to its first blockchain.

Advanced Proof Of Stake: Cardano

Cardano, a digital currency platform that is currently in development, (ADA) Cardano, the creator of ADA, a financial instrument that is similar to Gemini's, is creating ADA cryptocurrency. Cardano's protocol is expected combine privacy and scalability in the distributed ledger space.

ADA cryptocurrency was designed to be used in low-cost smartcards that can be embedded within a variety electronic products, such as smartphones or medical equipment. This will allow for real-time financial transactions as receipts. ADA developer and co-founder, ADA, stated that ADA is not just about currencies. He said that ADA was about creating the information flow in our marketplaces' distribution networks. ADA cryptocurrency is a bridge between the first and third-generation platforms.

Cardano's goal is to create blocks that are indistinguishable from existing networks, like MasterCard and Visa. Cardano is the co-founder of the Open Ledger Foundation. This foundation aims to build a backbone that can withstand censorship and protect the network. Cardano's founder, who is a doctorate holder in Computer Science and specializes in digital currencies, leads the Foundation.

One of the ADA features is its Proof of Stake system. It uses a special algorithm that distributes transaction fees among network users. This works in a simple way: users create blocks on their devices, which serve to show that they have the financial resources to sustain the network. Once the blocks are approved, they will be verified by a consensus algorithm. This will prevent network users from creating duplicate content, thus eliminating the possibility that centralization could occur. A proof-of–stake function will also enable currency users to get rewards for being members of the network.

ADA makes use of a technological breakthrough that consists of nodes that can receive and forward requests for blocks to one or several other nodes. Transactions are instantaneous, and the transaction are protected by multilayered security safeguards that keep them safe even if they're performed on the open market. ADO uses smart contractual technology to ensure the participants are able to agree to certain terms. There is virtually no chance of manipulation or interference from outside because transactions are distributed through smart contracts.

Cardano smart contracts are not required to be centrally administered because the Cardano protocol gives users the ability to earn rewards for creating new transactions blocks. Cardano protocols validate the validity of transactions by providing proof-of stakes. No third party is required to monitor and control Cardano. Cardano allows complete decentralization in administration, with a tamperproof digital signature program. Users can choose which software programs to run.

Cardano software is believed to be first to utilize homesteading because it uses new technology. The Cardano ecosystem allows tokens to be used at will. The Cardano platform is not a forced investment. This allows users of decentralized apps to decide what they feel most comfortable investing in.

Cardano is at this stage in its development. At the moment, it seems that Cardano's developers are working to expand upon the technology foundation. To make Cardano a viable competitor to Ethereum and Bitcoin, however, the project will need to overcome several significant hurdles. A major obstacle is the token base, which is still in experimental stages. Cardano is looking bright in the future.

What Are Stablecoins Anyway?

Stablecoins is a digital asset class which has assets values that are solely dependent on the US dollar's performance. This book covers Tether,

USD Coin (USDC), Binance USD (BUSD), three of the most significant stable coins that are backed by USD.

But that does not mean all coins on Binance's smartchain are US-backed. However, this is not the case. This means that you can purchase a Binance stable coin and have it backed in full or in part by the US dollars. A quote will be sent to you based on current spot prices once you make the purchase. The asset is now secured in US dollars.

This asset class does not come with a guarantee that you will use it or lose. This means that the Binance Exchange does not provide a loan for stablecoin purchases. It is unlikely that your ability to sell your stabilize coins will be significantly affected by the market's downturn (which sometimes happens). This is not the case for other virtual currencies. However, the risks and cost associated with stablecoins is quite different from those associated with altcoins.

Binance uses the Binance stablecoins to work customers' assets. It's very similar to how unsecured debt in the banking industry is handled. Once the customer has paid his money, he is often asked to stop spending the money and receive a check. Stablecoins let the customer purchase as many coins or as few as he likes until his balance reaches a maximum.

Ethereum and bitcoins don't have any fiat currency backing. The market movements that determine their value are the only thing that can affect them. Because of this, it's impossible to predict whether you will earn a profit on your purchase, particularly if the trade is short term. The same applies to all altcoins which are not stablecoins. The first are based on speculation as well as risk management and don't guarantee any type of liquidity. The difference is that stablecoin users enjoy price stability while other types of crytocurrencies prices can fluctuate widely.

Stablecoins are issued by an "interbank", rather than private lending institutions. This is unlike other altcoins. The US Federal Government enforces strict regulations on private lending institutions in terms their interest rates, and the maximum amount they are allowed to lend. There is little flexibility for brokers or the general public regarding the amount they are allowed to lend. These institutions must adhere to strict guidelines and are strictly regulated. This allows stablecoins to be more secure and reliable.

Stablecoins have many other benefits but these are two of the biggest. All investors should be aware. These listings include stable Cryptocurrency exchanges, high liquidity and long-term value links to fiat

US dollar. All these features are designed to give long-term profits for investors who make wise investments using stablecoins. As more investors see its advantages, the stable coins listed on these exchanges continue to increase.

Which stablecoins are best?

Stablecoins offer a stable and reliable alternative to traditional investment options such as certificates-of-deposit (CDs), individual savings account (ESAs), or money market mutual fund and stocks. These stable cryptosystems can be used to make flexible investments for both individuals and businesses. Stable coins can also be called stable money, tethers, or tethers. A stable coin does not lose its value as much as gold and is easy to sell when the market goes in the opposite direction. This type of investment offers low risk but high returns.

Many investors are attracted to the promise safe returns with high liquidity. As mentioned above, this asset type involves a digital asset that's traded between two parties over the Internet. This allows for quick funds transfers. There are many types of stablecoins available including silver and gold backed stabilitycoins as well precious metals and commodities backed steadycoins. Although this asset class can be attractive to many investors, only two types are most appealing to new investors. These include the stablecoins that are gold and silver-backed as well as those that are precious metals or commodities-backed.

Investors find stablecoins that are silver-backed attractive because they have high levels of stability. Stablecoins do not fluctuate in price as much, unlike gold and silver. As precious metals are required to guarantee their value, stablecoins with a backing are considered to be very secure. Investors who do not want to put too much of the assets they have at risk will find this stability attractive.

Precious metals and commodities-backed secure Coins are another type that stablecoins can appeal to a variety of investors. It is better to diversify than one's investments because this market is more volatile that the gold and silver markets. The market offers a wide variety of coins including gold and silver-backed safe coins and a range of coins like Eurozone Notes. This kind of stablecoins can be a great investment option for improving your portfolio because it is less risky then investing in gold or Silver.

These stablecoins are backed by several different countries. Stablecoins have been backed historically by the U.S.dollar. Today, the currency is being supported by several national and international governments. Canadian Maple Leaf offers support. Other countries that back stablecoins include the United Kingdom and the Netherlands.

These stablecoins have attracted many investors as they are a relatively safe investment vehicle. Stablecoins have many benefits that outweigh any risks. Stablecoins are supported by a national currency which gives investors the assurance that their investment will be protected in any economic downturn. This is not the case with many other currencies. Many lose value due financial crises or political instability. Investors often worry that their investment may lose value due to instabilities in the economy around the world. They therefore liquidate their holdings.

The low investment premiums that stablecoins have over other forms of investments is another benefit. Investors are taking advantage of the high cost of maintaining fiat currencies by investing in stabilitycoins. This is particularly true for those investors who have large amounts of capital which they could use to back their fiat money. In times like the recent economic crisis, European investors were financially wise to invest in U.S. dollar instead of relying only on their local currency.

It is important to evaluate both the potential benefits and risks of each stablecoin before you decide which one is the best. If you carefully examine these factors, you can determine if investing is the right choice for you. It is important to learn how you can start buying stablecoins once you have decided to do so. There are many methods to purchase this vital asset. The easiest is the "BTCUSDT" tether, also known as BTCUSDT. You can use a BTC Tether to gain access to the best stablecoins. It will also allow you to get started in this exciting new way to invest digitally.

Stablecoins are available for trade

The fiat currency-backed stability coins can also be backed by digital currencies. They are supported by a commodity which will provide long-term price stability. Stablecoins allow for traders to exchange currencies without having to worry about potential volatility. Stable coins are gaining popularity because they provide both the best of both, i.e. Instant transaction processing speeds and maximum privacy and protection for transactions of other currencies.

Two main categories of stablecoins are most commonly used by traders. The Money Trust, which is issued as a legal tender by the United States and can be used in Forex Trading, is the first. This financial instrument is guaranteed by the US government, though the list of countries that may have it might grow.

The Swiss National Bank issued the second major stable currency group, the peg Digital Currency. FCX does not have a physical counterpart, but is a virtual currency represented by a redeemable debit card. This card, which is linked to the Eurozone financial system, allows users to purchase Eurozone securities. They can also make transactions in the same manner as if trading were happening.

Although stablecoins are traded in many different forms, it is difficult for them to be compared to stocks or bonds. There is no physical asset that can be instantly converted into digital assets like a currency. StableCoins is a decentralized currency that does not have a central governing body. Its value is solely determined by its peg to fiat, commodity and the limited supply and demand in the market.

Since their inception, stablecoins have been used to make millions of trades. The stablecoins act just like traditional precious metals and can be digitally compared to precious metals such gold or silver. Instead of holding the metal in bullion coins or coins, investors typically buy them as smart contract with the central banks of the country where it is deposited. An investor can send a request at the central banking to have the coin transferred to him if he wishes to sell shares.

Chapter 8: Tether Currency And Commodity Indexes Can Be Investment Bridges For Crypto Investors

Tether is a stable currency cryptocurrency that is linked to US Dollar. Tether (money) can be backed by a security base. It could be the US Dollar, or any other global common money. Tether can trade like a futures agreement and be used as an alternate to the Euro, or the Swiss Franc. The abbreviation USDT can be used for tether that is linked to the US dollars.

Tether (USDT), though it is a cryptocurrency, is not typical. It is a Cryptocurrency Tie, which is backed US Reserve Asset and is worth 1 US dollar per token. Tether (money), which is not linked with any traditional asset class like stocks, bonds and commodities, is not tied to it.

Tether contracts provide rights to assets in the form of digitally signed certificates that can be used as tethers. They are also distributed to holders according a holder's entitlement. A holder refers to someone who is entitled one or more tethers. Tether awards a commission to each peer for his contribution in generating ether.

Sometimes the term "stablecoin", which is often used interchangeably to mean "cryptotether", is used. In the past ten years, "crypto tether" was used for any type of digital asset that could be backed or traded with non-traditional assets. Later, it was extended to any tradable "cryptotether", i.e. coins, papers, bonds, warranties, etc. The term "cryptotether" today refers any tradable property that is issued using a Crypto Currency (i.e. money) issued to an issuer which is not a bank or a government.

Tether was not created to be a stable cryptocurrency or as a hedge for speculative currency exposure. Tether Limited launched Tether Limited as a proofof concept to demonstrate its technology, and to attract developers and entrepreneurs. In hindsight this was a brilliant marketing move as it attracted attention about the lack of a profitable and secure tradable product. No one knew what a secure, tradable product could look like at that time. Tether was issued to act like an anchor in the market. It was only natural that people would want to find out what exactly it was.

Fiat Currency presents a number of problems. Because they are not backed up by credit cards power, the issuers depend on the public's opinion to continue issuing them. It is often inefficient and wasteful to create them. This is because the Tether price must be kept high enough to ensure that people buy into the base (the Tether), then use the Tether as leverage against any price rise. The entire system is dependent on speculation, not fundamental merits.

Tether is not the first token supported by USD that was launched. There have been many others before, but none that have had any impact. This new token will have a different backing. It is backed by actual physical commodities. The token will issue based on gold or silver and be traded on FX. The token won't be used for pump and dump schemes and will have a restricted trading volume. This is because it is obvious that trading physical commodities is the best place to speculatively trade.

Tether, a new service that's being launched, is an example. Other exchanges may also adopt it. It's a digital bridge between digital asset-backed currencies and fiat currency that is backed with actual commodities like gold or silver. This may prove to be a useful service in the future as it acts as a bridge between trading platforms.

Binance Coin - Altcoin Associate With a Crypto Exchange

Binance Coin (BNB), is an alternate currency or altcoin that is managed and maintained by Binance. Binance is a prominent online trading company. Binance. Binance provides a high-performance, electronic currency trading platform. Binance users are able to generate BNB interest or use it as payment fees to other trader.

Binance Coin can be traded anonymously using real money. Binance Coin can also be traded anonymously via pooled trading, which increases liquidity and reduces overall risk.

Binance is a great choice because it has low volatility and a relatively low trading volume. Binance coins can't be backed up by any government institution.

Binance Coins can also be traded the same as any other form of virtual currency. Smart contract technology enables traders to create an automated, self executing, real-time trading platform which automates all monetary transactions at the Binance exchange. Binance employs four types virtual money: Binance Cash virtual cash, Binance Gold digital currency, Binance tokens and Binance coin. Binance tokens do not have trading fees as they are backed up by real tokens such as the Euro. Binance Gold, which is backed with actual gold certificates is different.

Trading fees are applicable to every trade that costs the trader regardless of success. The volatility factor determines how much Binance trading fees will be charged. This complex formula calculates the volatility factor, which takes into consideration the start time and the end time of the period being analyzed. This formula will determine the market price of an asset for each period that Binance Coins were exchanged.

In a nutshell: Binance exchanges either peer to-peer(PPC) or futures trading platforms that are based upon one or more currencies. A peer to-peer Binance cryptocurrency exchange is similar in function to a stock market where trade transactions are made between buyers/sellers. However, a futures trading platform is not the same as a PPC. Brokers do not hold physical products. Futures exchanges are purely virtual. They allow traders to speculate about future price movements of assets, by agreeing on a purchase or sale of a specified amount of an asset at an agreed price and date.

There are four kinds of Binance Coin exchanges. The Binance Coin Market is the

Binance OTC Market; Binance Virtual Cash Markets and Binance Mutual Funds are the Binance Mutual Funds. Binance Coin Market allows you to trade popular altcoins such Litecoin and Dogecoin as well as the Binance Coin. Binance OTC Marketplace trades popular virtual currencies, such as the US Dollar (USD), the Euro, the Yen, or the Swiss Franc. The Binance virtual cash markets trade popular commodities. Binance Mutual Fund is an ETFX which is largely based upon stocks and options. This fund has a financial risk tolerance, primarily with futures and other options. Each of these four exchanges comes with a risk profile that can vary in the amount of return that each trade will generate.

Binance is a great platform if you are interested in investing in any one of the four major cryptocurrencysystems. Binance will enable you to easily analyze and identify profitable trades. It also allows you make profitable trades according to your own terms. Binance is among the first exchange platforms that allows clients to access the most popular and liquid cryptosystems. Binance will be a good platform to use for your investing plans as long as you are willing and able to invest time in learning about the markets.

Binance Smartchain

Binance Coin is an innovative virtual currency which can be used to trade fiat currency cryptocurrencies. Binance Coin exists to aid private traders and investors who are interested in investing into emerging cryptocurrencies. Continue reading if Binance Coin is of interest to you as an investor. This chapter will tell you more about Binance and the potential benefits it offers.

Binance Coin can be described as a new kind of virtual currency. It works in the same way that shares do. Binance Coin was issued by Binance. Binance is a large firm that allows investors, traders and institutions to participate in a network of transactions called the smart chain.

Binance Coin can still be used to trade, even though the platform is not affiliated with any major central currency. Binance utilizes three major exchanges. These exchanges provide liquidity, allow for maximum trading volume, as well as security. These three exchanges may not function in the exact same way as the US dollars or the Euro, but their trading volume and liquidity are comparable.

Binance coins are sometimes referred to also as tokens, virtual gifts, or tokens. To be able to participate on the exchange, you will need Binance account. Binance accounts are also known by eWallet, e Wagering and OTC wallets.

You can only buy and sell coins on the exchange. There are no face-to–face meetings. Binance Coin can be considered a virtual toy. Binance Coin cannot be purchased or held as a tangible asset. Binance differs from all other platforms because there aren't any utility coins that can be exchanged.

Binance smartboards are attractive to investors who have previously purchased Binance Coins as well to anyone intending to invest on the platform. The smartboard can provide financial services including money transfers and deposit and withdrawal services. It also offers investment options such as smart stocks, smart currencies, and other options like investing. With the smartboard, you can convert Binance Coins into virtually any virtual currency from the Binance smart coins ecosystem. These services can provide many benefits including fast conversions, low transaction costs, and lower trading commissions.

Binance's unique features have attracted attention. But it is important not to mistake it for the US dollars or the Euro. Binance is just a platform for trading in Cryptocurrency. On their website you'll see a list listing the countries where they have this service, so you can decide which one to do business. A link will take you directly to the signup page. Here you can complete your registration, and you can become a member of Binance. Individuals have found the Binance smart chain network a great way to convert their Binance tokens in other valuable currencies.

Ripple Protocol: Financial Institutions and Investors

It is important that you first learn about Ripple before diving deeper into this exciting new internet app. This chapter will help solve your problem.

Ripple, also known as XRP, is an Internet protocol which links two networks. It's called the protocol layer and the protocol network. The sending network can either be a peer-to–peer network (P2P), or an Internet backbone. The protocol layer is used to connect the two networks through a payment channel. This payment channel allows the networks to identify which asset they own when it's transferred between their systems. This is required for Ripple function effectively.

Ripple's mission is to simplify the process of exchanging money. Ripple works using a digital cashbot (XRP). Each transaction made on the ripple platform is assigned XRP. This is an attempt to create liquidity by allowing traders to trade without having to rely on one central exchange. Trader can trade directly with their private currencies. Many companies have adopted the idea of decentralized trading platforms, which is where ripple comes in.

One of the most effective uses of this new technology is for an asset owner to transfer ownership of a particular asset from their wallet to a broker who then transfers ownership to the asset. Private currency simply means that the currency you keep in your wallet is yours, not some digital asset. This concept is used by many thousands of companies. Financial advisors could profit from selling assets, and use the proceeds to purchase more appealing tokens.

This also means that an investment account is not necessary to participate with the asset transfer process. Because you won't be receiving a large percentage of the token's value, it makes no sense to have large deposits to trade on this market. If the market does not go well, you will not lose much money. These reasons are the main reason why financial institutions are using ripple for their investment purposes.

The ripple is the core of a tokenized economy. A financial advisor may begin to purchase domains of common tokens including gold and other metals, in hopes that they will appreciate. Once they have a comprehensive list, they can then open separate accounts on the ripple currency exchanges. Their goal is to acquire as many common tokens and lock in a small portion of the transaction price, all while trying to get as many as possible. Their goal: To leverage the power their real-time, gross settlement payment network.

Many banks have already started to use ripple as part of their transaction processing capabilities. Because it lets them take advantage their customers' realtime gross settlements and not have to rely on credit cards or other traditional systems like banks, this is why ripple is so popular. The tokens can be added a little value by banks, but they don't have to hold them as assets. They can also immediately use the tokens they receive from customers. This is known as interbank lending.

International money transfers are increasing in volume and banks need to be capable of processing large numbers of transactions. The interbank financing process helps to solve this problem. An escrow accounts allows banks to agree on the price of their common tokens. After that, ripple handles the conversion process. This escrow account is a way for banks to not rely on central ledger intervention, which can cause prices to rise drastically.

The distributed ledger protocol known as ripple is the ideal option for a money transfer network. Due to its system for international consensus, ripple is much more reliable than the current currency exchange methods. It's also transparent, which means both the sender or receiver of funds are able to see exactly what transactions have taken place. Distributed ledger technology is expected to be used in the future by all financial institutions for currency transfers that are secure and efficient.

Validation of transactions on XRP Market

Ripple, also known as XRP, is an alternative payment method (IPC) currently under testing. It's a cost-effective, worldwide settlement system that could reduce transactional costs as well as increase profitability. XRP is a form of digital cash that can be used in an unsecured manner. XRP doesn't use a credit rating system, which is why it can be used as a replacement for debit and credit cards. XRP does not require upfront payments, late fees, or excessive paperwork. Customers prefer XRP because of its speed and low cost.

XRP is a platform for digital payments that lets users convert currencies using a digital assets, also known "ripple currency". XRP can be used for the transfer of funds to traditional currencies such the US dollar or Euro, Japanese yen, and the British pound. XRP is available for trading on major electronic brokers. The Internet has made XRP widely available and is being used in many countries all over the world.

XRP was designed to provide small-business owners with an easy way to accept payment from their customers. Merchants can process transactions immediately, eliminating the need for intermediaries.

XRP can be used to attract new customers by retail outlets. It can be used to enhance brand recognition and raise exposure. Through advertisements and promotions, affiliates can introduce XRP to clients as well as potential customers. International money transfers can almost be instantaneously with the help of a well-designed campaign.

Many large financial institutions in America and Canada have been able, using Cryptocurrency, to process transactions totalling hundreds of millions of dollars. The largest beneficiaries of using XRP to transfer international money are the retailers who use the Digital Product Exchange for their customers to make local currency purchases. These retailers can use Cryptocurrency for remittances or other commercial purposes. They also get the benefit of using the Digital Product

Exchange for XRP to purchase for their businesses.

The value of the transaction remains the same regardless of whether the XRP is converted to Canadian or United States dollars. In the past, to buy XRP in order to establish a business, one would need to convert it manually into US Dollars. This is because the IRS considers all foreign currency transactions (including cryptocurrency exchanges) to be taxable income.

Dogecoin is a boon for cryptocurrency investors

Dogecoin, a digital currency favoured by marketers due to its low volatility levels and modest gains, has suffered some setbacks. This 'meme" coin is booming, however. Dogecoins are gaining popularity, which were once thought to be a joke coin.

Many entrepreneurs have begun to create new Dogecoins. Numerous websites offering Dogecoin trade have been created. Some of these new businesses operate as scams online while others are genuine businesses that aim to capitalize on the Dogecoin community's rising popularity. A fourth group called the DOGE Consortium issued statements declaring it was looking into ways to replace the current coins with the DOGE money.

So, what's the Dogecoin phenomenon? How did this obscure virtual currency which was not widely known outside the Internet bubble so quickly rise in value Is it because people in Silicon Valley are eager to join the new Internet moneymaker that is so popular? There are many possible answers to these questions, but all stem from the idea of a Dogecoin tipping level.

Dogecoin's rise to prominence began in April Fools' Day, when anonymous

Internet users promoted the crypto coin via popular blogs and forums. Soon, hundreds upon hundreds of dogecoins were traded each hour. Exchanges quickly began to pop up where traders could trade Dogecoins in accordance with their preferences. The frenzy lasted for several more weeks before one news story reported that high-profile Internet celebrities had bought millions of dogecoins. This was when the Dogecoin memes were formed.

It's clear why Dogecoin memes seemed so appealing.

But what is Dogecoin exactly? Dogecoin is a form cryptocurrency known as DOGE. It has been in the news recently. Dogecoin Cards are an offshoot to the original. The original featured a custom logo designed and created by an Australian cartoonist. Dogecoin memes utilize the same style of tweeting as the original users to make popular posts.

It works in a very simple way. Dogecoin works in the same way as other currencies. It uses a finite quantity of coins to establish a particular value. Each transaction is simply split into one of several possible denominations, and each denomination is assigned. The Dogecoin currency price, which is one of the most popular currencies, can be used to determine the cryptocoin's market performance.

It was, for example, a strong indicator that bullish sentiment was evident when the Dogecoin market price trended upwards in recent times. The Dogecoin then dropped on Elon Musk's speculative joking remarks. This was a sign that the uptrend had temporarily ended. Elon Musk later recognized the Dogecoin and it began to increase in value. This was a strong sign that the market was once more trending upwards. One individual's influence on certain low liquidity altcoins can be enormous. This is why investors need to be careful, particularly in the early days for new cryptocurrencies. The influence of celebrities and one individual will diminish as the cryptocurrency market matures. Because Dogecoins like Doge become more popular, so does their trading volume. Dogecoin will mature and its price should be less volatile over time. Once again, the whole market determines its real value.

Dogecoin has been a rising cryptocurrency in the last few weeks. Its marketing use to express the mood of the cryptocoin is what has attracted the attention of many within the business community.

Dogecoin Marketing Strategies to Improve Its Popularity

DOGE is Dog Cash. Although there are some smart investors who are familiar with it, many others are not. Programmers created it to have fun and create an ironic joke. Although it is funny, many people now consider it an online investment opportunity.

What is DOGE, exactly? Dogecoin (or Dogecoin) is an open-source digital asset and protocol designed for the Internet. It can be described simply as "a peer-2-peer virtual currency that replaces cash transactions." Please continue reading to learn more about this intriguing altcoin. Dogecoin founders refer to it as the "world's first virtual currency". It's also used as a Meme Coin, a novelty that has gained considerable popularity over the last year.

DOGE, which is a peer-to–peer virtual money, can be used to eliminate the need for real cash transactions. This makes it unique from many other Altcoins. Many use a Proof -of-work (POW), which provides proof that a transaction occurred. It removes the need for investors in mining for coins. This makes it transparent and allows for no chargebacks.

What makes DOGE different than other Altcoins available? Its creators created a new altcoin mascot, which bears a striking resemblance with an animated doggie on an animated children's TV series. The original mascot is the doggie. It is because the pink and black dogs are synonymous with street style and the cryptocurrency's high valuation makes it an attractive target for social media users and bloggers who want to make quick money.

Brains was also the creation of the founders dogecoin. They wanted to create a symbol that would be associated smart digital currencies. The mascot's head looks similar to a human. The face, however, is a druggie. A ponytail is often tied around his neck or back. His eyes are brightly green, which signifies the currency's colour. His tail reminds me of a black duffle bag, which is the symbol of the cryptocurrency's lackluster value.

DOGE's actual value is not in its image. DOGE was originally intended as a lighthearted gag. The low market value of this altcoin is the real value. Because it is not yet recognized by most merchants it is possible to purchase and sell it online on popular social media platforms. It's a safe investment that has no financial risks.

It is not well-known due to its low market price. It is also lacking the advertising power of many other cryptosystems. Dogecoin investors need not worry about the lackluster marketing. They have clever marketing options to drive interest in the cryptocurrencycoin. Offering giveaway items like wristbands or lanyards is one way to do this. These items will see a lot more use in the communities if they are well-received. The more dogecoin is exposed, the higher its value and the greater its worth.

DOGE does have an effect on bitcoin's market value, even though there is no advertising. If you consider the many rival currencies, the presence of a new cryptocoin could increase the market's liquidity. Bitcoins and dogecoin have a lot of similarities. Both bitcoins, as well as dogecoins, are popular for online casino payments. This coin is still quite new and it will be fascinating to see how it does against other competing coins.

Polkadot is a great option!

Polkadot aims to build an automated internet payment system for cloud computing. Polkadot is an open, shared heterogeneous multi-tier architecture. It allows multiple layer one and 2 "Paradigms", thereby creating a cloud-native Internet of blockchains. The network works with a consensus algorithm based on proof-of-stake (POS). The Data Channel, a bidirectional protocol for data channel protocols, allows the POS to be enabled. It comprises a bidirectional connector, gateways and storage.

Polkadot was created on the Ethereum protocol, as a solution provider to the open-source communities. The founders have a mission to create open-source software on the web. They include systems for application servers and database management as well as the networking fabric. Polkadot has existed since 2017.

Polkadot is known for its Relay Chain, Parachains and Parathreads as well as Bridges. Relay Chain oversees cross-chain interoperability and shared security.

Parachains, which are independent blockchains, can have their tokens running in the Polkadot system. Parathreads operate in the same way as parachains, but they use a pay-as you-go model. Bridges are also crucial in parathreads' and parachains' communication with outside networks like Bitcoin, Ethereum, and others.

Polkadot's tokenization system included multiple types of tokens. These tokens act as validators for ownership on the network. Five out of seven protocols that each had a specific color and meant one of seven things at launch were supported. Today, Polkadot tokens can be used in addition to seven of the original token types.

Polkadot offers an option for scaling. This feature is available as an add-on. This feature is called "metacoin." Metacoin is significantly stronger than other similar tokens, such as Polkadot.

Metacoin was built to solve problems in decentralized cryptocurrencies. Polkadot's purpose is to empower token holders to increase the market influence by giving them greater control over the total supply. The Polkadot token has been given a scaling option, which is expected to increase its market cap. The market cap increase will result in liquidity increasing which will improve the liquidity gap between capital and investors.

Increased market capital will likely lead to greater diversity in supply and demand. This will increase volatility in Polkadot's price. It will also allow the developers of these new cryptocurrencies based on Polkadot greater flexibility in defining new protocol rules. This will allow them the flexibility to improve the underlying asset and still meet their deadlines. Developers will likely increase interest in decentralized cryptocoins such as Polkadot if they meet their deadlines. This will result in developers being less concerned about technical issues and more focused on building a strong community around their project.

Polkadot's ability to adjust staking formulas is crucial for its long-term success. Cryptocurrency traders will be able to quickly adapt to new stake methods, which will enable them to trade with lower risks and potentially greater profits. While most ICO networks aren't adapting to the needs of investors today, Polkadot seems to have the potential to lead the way in developing crypto portfolios. Polkadot's cost will be competitive because of the large staking requirements to launch a successful ICO campaign.

This is why investors will be attracted and invest in the existing chains. Because of the inherent security and value Polkadot technology offers, investors may also wish to add Polkadot into their portfolio. Polkadot made significant strides even before it was launched in 2017. Polkadot founders quickly achieved their goal of 100% preICO financing. With more than $90k invested the first week and steadily increasing since, Polkadot is a revolutionary blockchain platform that has had a steady increase in market capital for many years. This is a sign that investors see the immense potential to buy Polkadot in co-development for the purpose of making the technology accessible to other chains.

Solana Core developers - Talks about how their Proof of stake model made a difference

SaaS's ecosystem is expanding rapidly. Microsoft, Apple, Salesforce, IBM and Apple have all created cloud services. It has been a long time since there was much discussion about how to scale SaaS platforms. Scalability is the ability of a platform to scale without changing its business models or users. Solana strives to eliminate these problems without compromising security or centralization.

Solana Labs launched Solana Labs' Solana ecosystem in March 2020. The Solana ecosystem is an innovative approach to verifying online transactions. This platform allows buyers and sellers to transact in real-time over the internet with minimal overhead. Many other projects struggle with slow speeds and high scaling. Although it may not offer the ideal environment for realtime data transfers this solution does promise to be more efficient and cost-effective during peak times.

To allow buyers and seller to transact on a network, each participant must create their own digital asset. This acts as a unique virtual key. Transactions are verified via the Distributed Leadger Interface (DLI). The Validator component is used to bridge buyers and sellers. This validates the transactions of each participant. The Validator acts as an intermediary to validate all transactions against the set of digital certificates on the ledger. Cryptographically protected, these certificates prove that all transactions made by participants are legal and fair in accordance to current network laws. Each certificate contains a link back at the original Distributed Ledger Interface.

Each validator generates proof that is stored in the ledger. The ledger can act as Byzantine consensus mechanism by storing the evidence. Each participant can establish independent keys to prove the fairness and legality of every transaction by creating multiple keys. As each proof is added to a ledger, the users have complete control of their money and private information. Once enough validators are connected the ledger will prove the validity and consistency all transactions. It also forms a trustable foundation for the entire system. This is Solana.

The proof/stake mechanism of slang is not the same as that of most blockchains. Since blockchains aim to keep transaction costs low, they also have the ability to stake. In order to protect their stake in the event that a transaction fails, users can stake a portion of the coins they have. Contrary to this, the proof/stake approach creates a baseline for each asset. It cannot be changed without changing its underlying value. The proof/stake protocol addresses concerns that users may have about their assets being abused.

Each node is a vote in the distributed system of solar. If a user verifies an asset's value, he gets a vote to validate his claim. Each round adds more solar cluster nodes until eventually, the network will be divided into hundreds or thousands individual ledgers.

There is no centralization risk as the distributed ledger is not centralized. Solana uses a consensus system to ensure that the ledger can function. This is in contrast to traditional blockchains which have some nodes controlling the majority of balance. The strong proof-ofstake mechanism in combination with the number allowed users to the network ensures that nodes are not able to collude to profit from the power of honest users.

Because the Solana protocol uses proof of work (POW), attackers cannot take control of the network or make unlimited transfers of funds. He could easily double spend existing assets if this were possible. Each transaction in a solar network transaction is unique. They are all timestamped and stored in a blockchain. When you make a commitment to do business together, you also create a transaction in Blockchain with him. This shows that you have agreed on terms and are fully aware of what the transaction entails.

Chapter 9: Solana: The New Crypto Competition

Solana, a new digital currency, intends to replace all old money as well as paper checks by its own highly secure digital currency. It doesn't require you to have any prior knowledge, unlike other digital currency. It depends entirely on its user community for smooth operation. The currency is not centralized and serves the individual needs of each community.

Solana uses smart contract technology to host decentralized apps. Solana's operation is based on different parameters. This allows it to offer lower transaction fees, while increasing the rate for the network. The Proof-of-Concept method was used by the developers. This system combines three well-known components - iControl, IaaS, and Transaction Scalar Networks. Combining the three components creates what cryptographers refer to as a "safe" environment that ensures security without compromising system security. It means that users can perform secure transactions instantly and in one click.

Solana uses a proof of work (POW), which generates blocks times that are guaranteed. This is in contrast to other digital currencies, like Zcash or Dash. The proof-ofwork approach is preferred because it increases the chances that a new Node will be added to a network. This results in fast, secure transactions. PoCs at launch were not performing well in PoW, so their assumption that faster block times will result in more users turns out to be false. Furthermore, this system allows truly decentralized scalability.

The main problem facing businesses that want to use ethereum to raise funds is its dependence upon centralized exchanges. Decentralized networks, like the one proposed by its creators, would ensure fair distribution among distributors, investors, and lenders. But centralized exchanges make this system heavily dependent on a handful of large players. If one of these players goes bankrupt, all the others will cease to exist. This presents a serious threat in the development of the decentralized altcoin group.

Solana's creators solved this problem with a decentralized validater mechanism. The decentralized validation system, which is not like a regular validater, ensures that only the holders for a particular transaction are included on the validated database. In other words, each time someone requests a validation, the request is sent out to all validators. Any changes are made to the participants' list accordingly. Only then can the request be approved and the list validated. This system, while it sounds complicated, greatly reduces the risk of any particular group manipulating this list. It could also break the distribution chains and potentially harm the entire cryptocoin ecosystem.

Solana has created a strong staking scheme to ensure tokens that are obtained through the staking process do not go towards any other projects. These parameters include criteria for determining how many tokens are distributed and how the tokens are allocated. Tokens will allow participants to convert their assets in actual currency, maximising their potential return.

What is UniSwap and how does it work

Uniswap, a blockchain-based alternative to the traditional exchange, allows anyone to trade digital assets using a smart contracts. It offers several advantages over traditional forex trading platforms:

you can trade via a virtual online account, trade almost any altcoin/cryptocurrency pair at any time, and you can personalize your risk/reward profile. Best of all it is free from a broker. It doesn't require any software to use or maintain any websites.

The original Uniswap Protocol was released in November 2018. New features are continually added to it. These include higher leverage levels as well as faster transaction processing and liquidity. The Uniswap V3 is due to be released in 2021.

One of the most important aspects of the Uniswap-decentralized exchanges' increased liquidity is. The Uniswap decentralized exchange does not employ a broker so you can instantly access real-time quotes for all major altcoins. It is decentralized and you won't have to worry if third parties charge high transaction fees. You'll be able cut these costs by doing all your business transactions yourself. The liquidity will allow you to trade more often, increasing your profit. This feature has significantly improved the performance Uniswap.

Hayden Adams is an automated program that is part of the Uniswap protocol. This automated trading platform is designed to quickly react to market movements and produce profitable trades. Trader's can reduce the risk of currency holdings that have declined in value because the automated system relies on real-time quotes provided by Uniswap. Additionally, the automated system is based only on Ethereum blockchain smart contracts that cannot be upgraded, which improves the validity, accuracy, and reliability of the Uniswap markets.

You can visit the official Uniswap webpage to view the interface. This allows you to navigate to the decentralized currency exchange by updating prices for swap tokens.

Uniswap is an open source decentralized platform. This is what makes trades in the system possible. Traders may choose to open a brand new trade by clicking the "New Trade" button. This opens a screen where the trader can specify the asset to be traded (the currency pair chosen by Uniswap). Then they click "Trade". Next, they click on "Trade".

ERC-20 tokens will be used for uniswap trades. These tokens are based the Ethereum blockchain's real-time transaction price. ERC-20 tokens used to trade in Uniswap are transferable and not limited in availability.

Uniswap - A Hybrid Investment platform

Uniswap, a unique way to transfer funds in Cryptocurrency is a concept that was developed by OLP members. Uniswap is a distributed network of brokers that allows for the transfer of funds between investors or traders. Uniswap does not restrict users from trading through brokers and exchanges. Instead, it allows anyone to perform all financial business within the same network. This allows anyone or any company to trade in the volatile Cryptocurrency market. This chapter will give more information on the Uniswap project, and explain how it differs from other Cryptocurrency protocols.

Uniswap's token-issuing design is one of its biggest advantages over other popular protocols. Uniswap is a token system that works in place of a currency exchange. Users can quickly exchange tokens without the need to use conventional exchanges. The token system serves as the digital currency account unit. This new method allows users to manage and monitor their finances through a decentralized network.

The Uniswap program allowed brokers to offer clients more functionality through the launch. Uniswap's software has been enhanced with several new features that will further improve its utility. These include the ability, among other things, to manage multiple token accounts, to track and manage your funds each day, and to transact on Ethereum. Today, the protocol is available as a v3 upgrade that adds the following features.

Uniswap's efficient distribution model is one of its best features. A distributed ledger system offers many advantages for any program, including scalability as well efficiency and reliability. Traditional ledgers used to track funds in traditional blockchain environments require large bandwidth and huge storage space. Uniswap uses a different approach to managing the distributed ledger. Instead of each ledger having its block or series blocks, the entire process takes place on a proof–of-stake basis. Each investor will be limited in their ability to create accounts with the collateral of a given value.

Uniswap also features a hybrid smart-contract protocol called the ERC-20 protocol. This makes it stand out from other Cryptocurrency networks programs. Investors and traders have the option to use tokens as a digital asset for transaction funding and risk management. Investors can avoid fines and restrictions by using tokens instead real money.

Uniswap also integrates social trading, which is a unique feature that makes it stand out from other top down Cryptocurrency programs. Contrary to some Cryptocurrencies, which restrict traders' ability to transact within their network, Uniswap allows users to interact with each other and build their networks through the same platform. This can increase liquidity and thus, the demand for tokens. In fact, many new names in the Cryptocurrency trading area have emerged following the announcement about Uniswap. These people are all competing for the right to profit from Uniswap.

Uniswap uses tokens to create value. This is the biggest draw. Uniswap has created an open-source platform for users to exchange tokens. This allows them to provide liquidity without the restrictions of centralized exchanges. Uniswap is free from trading fees. Traditional exchanges can impose huge trading fees on traders. Uniswap users are able to enjoy a passive source of income in addition to eliminating the fees.

Finally, users of the Uniswap exchange platform will enjoy the enhanced security that comes from being part a decentralized exchange. The token-based financing system provides users with a cost-effective and flexible way to secure capital. Uniswap is able to react faster to market changes and increase liquidity by decentralizing trading. Uniswap created a unique hybrid private-equity investment model by combining a token-based finance system with increased liquidity.

Learn more about Bitcoin Cash (BCH).

Figure: Notice the sign that states Bitcoin (not Bitcoin Money). Many novices mix these together. Bitcoin Cash (BCH), while promising, is not the original Bitcoin. Don't mistake altcoins (BCH), for the original Bitcoin (BTC).

Cryptocurrency is money that can be stored and traded electronically. Bitcoin is the most famous example. People can quickly convert one currency to another, or use their funds to purchase another currency without needing to wait for the traditional payment method to change.

Two elements are essential to Cryptocurrency: Digital Asset, and Financial Asset.

Bitcoin Cash's developers made the decision to fork Bitcoin Cash due to a variety of reasons. Most notable was the perception of not enough fees being paid for users who had moved to the new fork. The developers believed that this was due to bitcoin cash's lack of real value. BIP 11 was created as a code to change how fees are paid. This code was then released and Bitcoin Cash's network split into two separate factions.

Miners are responsible for securing the network. They also decide how much money they will invest in the system. BIP 13, a new block-based system, decides who miners are and what they pay to join the network. Core Developers are Software Developers and Full-Service Providers have an interest.

Core Developers, who are responsible for writing the majority of the code that is the backbone and the software, are also developers. They make decisions regarding code modifications and how they can be integrated with the community. Core Developers' purpose is to ensure the safety, security, and value of decentralized ledgers that are used as the backbone in the entire bitcoin cash system. Core Developers will handle any problems that arise in the system. Their job is to ensure that all users are safe from any possible problems caused by the protocol modifications.

Individuals who create software tools necessary to implement the features in Bitcoin Cash are another group interested in Bitcoin Cash. These tools will be then submitted to miners for their use in mining operations. The software developers' main goal is to help miners earn more. Miners can increase the amount of cash they mine, as well as reduce their expenditures. They act as intermediaries between users of the system and the decentralized ledger.

The Full Service Provider group, which is its name, will handle all the necessary services for the deployments of the new blocks. These services include building and maintaining the mining equipment and ensuring that the client's software applications work with the new blocks. Security is a critical aspect of the network. This can make it difficult for them to keep up with the latest developments. In addition to creating new blocks, these entities also have to supervise their workers.

The best thing about the bitcoin cash system, however, is that anyone can conduct all of their activities within it without having to rely upon a third-party.

The system can manage transactions between multiple people who have an account using the digital currency. The community known as bitcoin cash was responsible for the creation of the technology. These individuals wanted to create an easy way for ordinary consumers to spend their money with a new electronic cash.

It is important for people to realize that this type technology is not meant to replace the real-world system. The bitcoin protocol is an alternative currency that aims to increase economic freedom. It is their goal that everyone can use their money freely and without any hassles.

BCH is a stable and reliable Bitcoin fork

This chapter will explain more about altcoins and Bitcoin Cash. In this chapter, we will be looking at the history of the Altcoin, including how it was first traded on various currency exchanges. Its future potential as an attractive investment vehicle and whether or not it has proven to be a viable alternative.

Let's begin by taking a look at bitcoin cash's history. It was the result of two companies working together to provide an alternative to mainstream currencies traded on online exchanges. Their idea was to make transactions faster and lower the cost of on-chain data transfers. They wanted "simplify" how trades are made on the chain.

SegWit is the new technology that was developed by the team. It solves two problems that were previously present with the older alternatives. Scalability was the second problem. Because of scalability, smaller blocks were possible to hold higher volumes. This was necessary to allow for increased block sizes without affecting performance.

SegWit solved the second problem of increased block sizes. The average transaction size for SegWit is 2.5MB. This will increase as more users adopt the new protocol. Scalability will also become a concern. SegWit technology can be used to implement a larger block. This will allow for greater transaction processing speed while still maintaining high scalability.

But if you don't understand the details of how the hardfork was created, you might not understand why scalability is so important to the new cryptocurrency. The forks that are created must both be stable and secure. If the other fork is rejected, it will be replaced. Bitcoin Cash was no different. However, they needed to prevent any long-term harm that a single fork could cause.

The hard fork has opened up new opportunities for the entire industry. The rise in alternate currencies' value is something you must be aware of.

You need to stay up to date with all the latest news regarding different blockchains. So you don't get caught out and trade against it, you must know how the ecosystem and protocol react to any changes. Although crypto coinage's future is unknown, investors remain excited about its potential. However, the future is still far away and the hard work that has been done is just one step closer towards changing the landscape.

What's next for bitcoins and altcoins? It's safe for us to say that although the future looks bright, it is not yet clear what lies ahead. For those who have waited for a safe return on their investment, however, the bright future most investors see is good news.

Litecoin continues to be one of the fastest-growing altcoins

Litecoin, also known as LTC, is a peer-to-peer Cryptocurrency. The project was released under an open license. Litecoin started in 2011, as a spinoff of Bitcoin. Litecoin uses a modified proof of work system, also known as proof of stake. This is a major difference from most cryptocurrencies. To prove work, each person who will be participating in the network receives a certain amount Litecoin. This award can be referred to in various instances as a "stake" or cap.

Litecoin was the fastest-growing virtual currency in the world by 2021. This was mainly due to the lack of fundamental problems in supply or demand for Litecoin. Its value has increased to over 100 dollars in the 10 years since its initial launch.

The popularity explosion of Litecoin has led to an increase its supply. This peaked at more than 25 percent. This was primarily due Litecoin Testnet which was released by its developers. Litecoin Testnet (closed source program) allows users the opportunity to test the functionality and various aspects the Litecoin protocol. Users may use their personal computers to test Litecoin, and connect via the Internet to the testnet network. The Testnet is a portal that allows individuals to connect to the main Litecoin server without taking a risk.

The popularity gained by Litecoin eventually led it to be included in the main Litecoin leadger, also known as the blockchain. Litecoin can now be traded worldwide as any other cryptocurrency. Decentralized infrastructure known as the blockchain could allow instant global trades. This is an attribute that is missing from the centralized blockchain.

One unique feature of Litecoin makes it different than other cryptocurrencies is that it recognizes that the less a transaction has been made, the more money a marketmaker is able to capture. Litecoin also has a unique incentive system which allows it implement a "mining" function. Litecoin miners receive a reward based on how difficult it is to generate new blocks. Litecoin miners who join the pool more often will have a higher difficulty level and therefore, the possibility to produce new units.

Litecoin's initial circulating supply was around twenty-four thousand coins. The circulating supply of Litecoin has now reached sixty-sevenmillion. The market demand may change the number of circulating coins. This figure does not reflect the unconfirmed holdings of

Litecoins. The total supply is capped at 84,000,000 LTC. This figure is comparable to Bitcoin's 21,000,000 BTC limit. Litecoin's supply is capped, which is similar to Bitcoin and many other altcoins mentioned in this book. (In contrast, stablecoins like USDT are not deflationary as they are linked with fiat currency. The stablecoin supply will need to increase each time governments print more fiat money.

Litecoin was valued at nearly 12 million dollars as of the publication date.

Litecoin is the Original Crypto 'Silver.

Litecoin, also known as LTC, is an open-source and peer to-peer digital currency and asset. Litecoin (LTC) was an early experiment in Bitcoin's spin-off. It was created in October 2011. It was known as'silver' during the early days when Bitcoin was analogous to gold. Litecoin, however, has a few competition for the 2nd spot (silver). Litecoin continues to be a valuable altcoin and has shown its value over time.

The network allows users to exchange and sell their litecoin. Litecoin can therefore be considered an alternative to virtual money, such as prepaid credit cards and online shopping systems.

Litecoin differs from most other currencies in that it does NOT handle liabilities. This is a great advantage for investors starting out, who don't want to own large amounts of unmonetized assets. Litecoin transactions do not need to be tied to any one currency. Unlike many altcoins, there are no regulations. This is another advantage for new investors, who might not like the idea of investing their funds in centrally controlled countries that can make money transfer slow and complicated.

Another advantage to Litecoin is the anonymity of its trading through what is called a "mixer network". This is accomplished by a specialized program that registers individual Litecoin address and then mixes the coins to be traded. An investor must have a private secret key in order to log onto the Litecoin Mixer Server and access the market. Once he gets there, he can receive his funds. Also, the transaction will appear on the Litecoin ledger. This system prohibits any direct interaction between individual investors. Litecoin is therefore attractive to private investors.

Litecoin offers a significant advantage in that transactions take only 2.5 minutes. Because it uses a quicker network than the main Bitcoin networks, and also has a shorter hops protocol, Litecoin takes only 2.5 minutes to complete transactions. It's worth noting that this is much shorter than the 8 to 10 minute average transaction time required by main Bitcoin network.

Litecoin is one of the original contenders. It has been closely following Bitcoin for a decade. The future may see a surge in altcoins based upon the Litecoin Open-Source Code, which, in turn, is an original Bitcoin derivative. However, for now we will need to wait and see how the previous cryptocurrencies tried to mimic Litecoins. They eventually disappeared. Other altcoins built using other networks will also attempt to compete with the originals.

Chainlink Smart Contracts Hybrids

Chainlink (LINK), a virtual token based on Ethereum, acts as a backend link to internal data sources, APIs and payment methods. This network allows smart devices on the Ethereum network to connect securely to external third-party APIs, data sources, and internal payment system without having to expose any sensitive information. This network allows for a secure real-time connection to be established between multiple smart contracts programs. It uses an encrypted channel. Smart contract programmers are able to access multiple types of data, channels, and resources without restriction, which is crucial for creating highly interactive online business models.

Users participate in Chainlink just like any token decentralized oracle networks by asking for nodes that join the network at a specific time. These nodes, called "chainlinks", are made up of 5 billion chains. When one of these links is complete, other nodes join a queue. The whole system then becomes self-sustaining and self-guarding Byzantine Fault Tolerance Network (BFT). If malicious nodes attempt to connect to the network, this Byzantine fault tolerance system will kick in and all transactions will stop until they are removed.

Chainlink, which is the token used to create the system, is mined on the Ethereum network. A distributed distribution system ensures that tokens are distributed evenly by using an algorithm that guarantees that the same people participate in the creation of each new Chainlink. Chainlink does NOT have any centralization. The unlimited supply of Chainlink tokens is similar to other currencies. It's possible to create new tokens quickly and cheaply. Because there is a limited supply, the supply can be constrained by the amount of tokens distributed to businesses and individuals.

The whole process is easy: Nodes that take part in the Byzantine Fail Tolerance process either buy or return tokens from other participants in the system. After each transaction is complete, the seller of the token will receive a fixed percentage plus any fees. A distribution point of approximately one trillion tokens is theoretically possible. This would give an ICO token a value of thousands of US dollars. This is dependent on whether or not there is a regulatory body added to the Cryptocurrency Act.

Many of those who have chosen to take part in the ICO craze hope to become successful traders, and that the market cap increase will enable them to realize financial independence. Some see the trend simply as a bubble and will not be able to profit from it soon enough. They see the rising value currencies as an opportunity to make money from the "tulip" effect. One speculator could be able to receive five Tulips per two hundred thousand.

Investors who are joining the chainlink wave are finding that it is easy to trade anonymously. It's possible to open an account that allows you gamble on altcoins, as long as you buy from the main pool. It isn't the most ideal way to get involved in the ICO hype if you want to use a stable coin, but it provides anonymity.

Chainlink does have some disadvantages for beginners.

Most people don't think about the difficulties of setting up wallets or accessing private keys when considering investing in Cryptocurrencies. Due to the recent revelations about the theft of confidential information belonging Chainlink traders, it is even more important that you learn how to manage and secure your private key. If you protect your private keys, you'll have no problems transitioning to the new altcoin markets. It is important to look at how the protocol works when investing in Cryptocurrencies and Altcoins. Chainlink is one example of an altcoin that is newer than the rest, but the protocol being used is not only more advanced than the other altcoins in this category. There is always room to innovate in any industry, so it is likely that altcoins such Chainlink will continue growing as the technology behind their development matures.

Chainlink to Support Your Cryptocurrency Program

Chainlink (LINK), a virtual currency based on Ethereum, enables Chainlink digital public blockchain. This public database is a duplicated interactive database, where all transactions can be logged and securely recorded. Transactions are executed along the same chain which ensures that they can be confirmed and executed immediately. Smart contracts allow for money transfers and other business purposes. This system allows for secure, scalable, permission-protected, and distributed collaboration.

Chainlink dramatically expands the capabilities and usability of smart contracts, providing access to real data and offchain computing. However, it maintains the reliability & security that is the hallmark of blockchain technology.

Chainlink developers' main focus was to develop a better system for digital contracts, including smart contract platforms that work with public networks. The team developed and built hundreds of smart oracles, based on open-source projects. Numerous smart oracles were already in production and are being deployed across different locations around the world.

Chainlink consists of two major components. Chainlink tokens or sets ether and other digital currency, and Chainlink application oracles. The tokens, or ether, are the core of the system. Other components such as the application Oracles add functionality. Tokens can be used for services purchased from outside companies. These services are then indirectly reflected into the value the ether. Chainlink smart transactions ensure that the transactions can be executed immediately.

There are several types available for the Chainlink smart contract. The original Chainlink system was composed of two types. The "parent" set of nodes is the first. These nodes are responsible to spread the information among all the connected nodes. This second type is known as the "child", node.

The Chainlink protocol was improved upon by its developers. The developers have created a new type smart contract that gives you greater privacy. To send the transactions, the new feature uses dummy servers to do so without broadcasting them to other networks. This is the "blockchain-oracle" version of Chainlink.

However, over the past years, the developers were able to successfully combine the ideas of the original Chainlink and the most recent innovations on the market.

Next, let us discuss each of these Chainlink elements. The tokens serve to represent Off-Chain Sources. The smart contract then transfers the tokens from OnChain Sources to the buyers. Let's also talk about the usage of Chainlink data that is provided by the smart-contract.

It is important to observe the work of the off and on-chain chains. One thing that must be remembered is that smart contracts can use any technology, but users still need to comply with the basic rules set forth in the chainlink. It is important not to perform unnecessary transactions, or link chains without sufficient backup information. Off-chain systems offer many advantages, including privacy, control, and security features. However, users need to be careful not to misuse them.

Many functions can be performed by token sellers and buyers, such as accessing other smart contract, accessing the underlying data feeds and recording the addresses and transactions of other participants. Chainlink is protected from denial-of service attacks, as all messages are broadcast over the wide network. Decentralized oracle networks, which are internets that consist of many IP networks, protect token buyers against these attacks. By using this decentralized oracle system, users are protected from all attacks, during or after the execution of the smart contracts.

Sellers and buyers who are smart contract buyers need to be sure that there is no double-spending. Chainlink users need to make sure they have enough research and development done before they begin their Chainlink project. If their projects take off, they can easily realize profits without the need to resort to any tricks.

Chainlink is the place to go if you're interested in getting involved in the exciting worlds tokens, smart contracts and smart tokens. Chainlink's tokens and trading prices are not influenced by other currencies or commodities. They are only affected by the performance and results of the projects they represent. You can immediately gain profit by taking part in these projects and helping to grow the industry. Additionally, these projects do not involve any currency or physical cash, which means that the risk of losing money is significantly reduced. Chainlink is a good option for anyone wanting to create a business within the digital economy.

HOW TO INVEST IN and STORE ALTCOINS

In this section we will show you some cryptocurrency exchanges where it is possible to buy bitcoins and other emerging cryptocurrencies. We'll also be discussing the best ways to store them for safekeeping.

What are the Most Popular Cryptocurrency Exchanges in Common?

These online exchanges offer clients the ability to trade fiat currency and virtual currencies for cryptocurrencies, or other virtual currencies. With the rise in the crypto market, their popularity has increased. This industry has attracted many prominent businesses as well as large financial institutions.

These services are described in detail below. The typical marketplace contains several monetary units. These can be either owned by users, traded between users, or held by the marketplace. The software platform used for the transfer of these currencies is typically designed specifically for this purpose. There are many currencies that can be traded on these platforms, including Bitcoin, Ethereum, as well as the Altcoins described in this book. These are some of the more well-known and stable currencies traded on Crypto Exchanges.

These platforms have several advantages over the traditional, over-the-counter market. They have increased liquidity, which allows for more buyers to potentially influence the market. Traders can now make better predictions about market movements and take advantage of lucrative opportunities to make more money.

To choose the best platform, you need to first understand what your needs are. You might want to trade higher-quality coins or larger quantities, so it is important to choose a trusted and established platform. Consider the liquidity provided by your broker as an important factor if you are looking for freedom to trade and exit the market at will. To make sure you are comfortable trading with real money, it is a good idea to request access on demo platforms if you are new to crypto exchanges.

Demo accounts on a crypto exchange are advantageous because you can trade with fictitious assets without risking real money. Some demo platforms seem very realistic. Before you get enough practice, double-check that it's a demo account and not a real one. A basic understanding of cryptocurrency will be necessary if you want to trade large or high-interest coins. You'll become more familiar with the market as you trade cryptocurrency.

Trading cryptocurrency could be a topic for a whole other book. This is because it is a very advanced topic. This book focuses more on investing than trading. Altcoins of greater quality are emphasized, as they can be valuable investments.

The marketplace will see many regulatory changes in the coming months and decades. Many of these regulations will be implemented in the United States. Some will also be implemented in England. Additionally, there are other regulatory changes that can be expected all around the world. Any regulatory changes to cryptocurrency exchange trading platforms are necessary in order to meet their customers' needs. They will have to adapt their services to accommodate the regulatory changes, and allow the market access to unscrupulous digital currency exchange businesses.

Cryptocurrency Exchanges require potential members to pledge safety and privacy. Both customers and service providers desire their information to be kept private and protected from outside influences. This is one reason why Cryptocurrency Exchange investors are willing spend large amounts of money on these types services. Cryptocurrency users will need to be protected more by regulators in the future.

Conclusion

A decade has passed since the introduction of cryptocurrency. The market is flourishing because ambitious investors are now able to invest in these digital coins and make a fortune.

The Bitcoin was not the first gold coin to be traded, but there are many alternative cryptocurrencies that can also be traded on cryptocurrency platforms. This is what has made these digital transactions so successful.

The Ethereum, Litecoins, Ripple, and the original Bitcoin are just a few of the most widely used cryptocurrencies. Investors can choose from a variety of coins to maximize their chances of multiplying their hard-earned funds.

After deciding the amount they are willing risk in this business, an investor must create a crypto portfolio. During this time, investors need to decide which specific coins they will be putting at risk.

For easy tracking of their losses and profits, the risk-takers must have a cryptocurrency wallet before they can enjoy their investment.

The digital wallets are not the only tools that are available for managing investors' portfolios. They can also be used to assess whether or not they are making any profit. Many tools can be downloaded and used to manage the portfolio. Different users pick the app that best suits their needs.

You need to make sure you know which exchanges you can use to buy the cryptocurrency you desire, despite all of this information. There are many ways to buy the coins that you wish to invest in, including using cash or cashless systems.

Unfortunately, not all of the economic analysts' findings discourage investors from investing in cryptocurrencies. To minimize the risk and maximize the profits, you should conduct extensive research on which coins to invest in, as well as which exchanges are most favorable to trade them.